Passive investing on steroids

Using leverage to reduce risk and increase returns

Daniel Fernandez Ph.D.

Disclaimer

The contents of this book are provided for educational purposes only and do not constitute investment advice. All past performance shown is hypothetical and does not represent actual real past trading results. **Past performance, either real or hypothetical, does not guarantee future results**. Please consult with your own financial adviser to discuss the risks and possibilities of the investment methodologies described in this book before you consider applying them to real money. Although all the contents of this book are provided in good faith, are applied actively in my live trading and have been checked for accuracy to the best of my knowledge I take no responsibility for any mistakes that might be present within them. Please make sure you double-check any results contained herein to ensure they are accurate to your satisfaction. I am only human.

Table of Contents

Disclaimer..2
Introduction...4
   Who this book is for..4
   What you will learn...5
   Exchange Traded Funds...7
   Looking at charts...8
   Comparing different investment portfolios...9
   A note about portfolio allocations and re-balancing..11
   The R code appendix...12
Leverage...13
   Introduction to leverage...13
   Types of leverage...13
   Leverage and compounding...18
   The risks of using leverage..19
Leveraged Passive Income Portfolios..21
   Introducing bond and stock portfolios...21
   A note about bond/stock relationships..25
   Choosing a stock ETF using capitalization...25
   Choosing a bond ETF..29
Monitoring portfolios and timing investments..35
   Analyzing your portfolio...35
   Drawdowns and investing...38
   Notes about risk and risk tolerance...40
Conclusions..42
R code appendix...44

Introduction

Who this book is for

If you asked a thousand people what they would ideally want from their investments they would all answer the same thing. They would all want investments that gave the highest possible returns over time, with no losses and without having to spend any time thinking about them. In simple terms, high, steady, hands-free returns. Sadly in the real world this is not possible and we generally have to compromise over the characteristics of the ideal investment. We can have something hands-free and steady at the expense of returns, something steady with high returns at the expense of time or perhaps something hands-free with high returns at the expense of stability.

The first option above focuses on people with low risk tolerance, the second focuses on people with ambition and time and the third focuses on people who have a long time horizon for investments. People in the first group will generally go for financial instruments like government bonds while those in the second group are likely to study successful investors like Warren Buffet or Benjamin Graham and attempt to put a lot of time and effort into making their investments in the smartest ways possible. The third group of people will often be those with no time or desire to care for the specifics of investments, with higher ambitions but little concern over short-term risks. This group will generally invest in things like stock indexes or similarly higher yielding instruments.

Of course there are those who want to have their cake and eat it too, those who want to achieve the ideal investment where there are high, steady and hands-free returns. In this group you will usually find very high failure rates. This is a consequence of the nature of high and steady returns as this result demands a very significant edge over the market that cannot magically appear. Failure to invest this time and effort will tend to yield poor results. Moreover the level of time and effort needed is often under-estimated so people easily fail because of an effort that just wasn't big enough.

This is especially true in the case of shorter term traders, people who attempt to beat the market by making weekly, daily, hourly or even minute by minute predictions of where certain market instruments are headed. Imagine a pool filled with sharks with one coin at the bottom of it, the person who gets the coin would be the one who made the biggest effort to get there. If you are the only one there you might be able to get there with a lot of effort and patience but if there are another 10 thousand trying they might out-smart you very rapidly so you will need to think faster and smarter to get the same reward. The level of effort needed increases as more people seek the same rewards. It is very easy to underestimate the effort needed to get to that point and that is the reason why failure statistics among traders are so dismal.

Don't get me wrong, there will always be Simons, Buffets and Grahams among us and I definitely would encourage those who want to get very high and steady rewards at the expense of their time to go into this direction. I have done so as well and the rewards can be incredible but the amount of hard work and effort should not be under-estimated. The journey can indeed be very satisfying for those with the personality traits and drive necessary to achieve these goals. However my book is not addressed at people in this group. My book is not for those who want to delve deep into market instruments or companies and trade or invest in the smartest possible way. This book is aimed at people who want more from their passive investments without having to spend any time per week or month doing investment management, it's for those who want a set-and-forget way of investing that is likely to out-perform the market in terms of returns and risk without having to spend time looking at their investment portfolios.

It's also important to note that this book is therefore not about the smoothest ride or the highest returns. The book is about providing a better approach to passive investment using tools that are rarely used for this purpose (due to their higher level of perceived risk, which I will go into in chapter 2). It is about getting better returns with lower risk in a hands-free way, a way for people in the third group of investors to get a bigger bang for their buck without having to spend any large amount of time in the investment world.

If you have an investment portfolio or would like to start investing and you want to do this in a smarter way but you have no desire to spend a ton of time doing analysis then this book is for you. This book is for the average Joe who just wants passive investments on steroids, a way to boost rewards and reduce risks using a smart yet hands-free investment approach. My book does not want to turn you into the next great legendary investor out there, all it wants is to help you increase your returns and shorten the time needed to reach your financial goals using the tools that are available to retail investors that I use myself. Tools that are already used by investment management firms and hedge funds to increase returns for their clients.

It is also worth noting that my book does not assume a lot of investment knowledge from the reader so I will try to cover a lot of basics that are usually covered in introductory investment books. I will do so in a practical way, trying not to overwhelm readers with excessive complexity. Although the book does not require the user to know anything about complex math or coding it does include some resources that might be helpful in the tracking and assessment of the portfolios covered within it. In this manner those of you who wish to go deeper will be able to reap an additional benefit from these tools.

What you will learn

Now that we've covered who this book is for we can now go into the details of what we will learn through this journey. Within this introductory section I will start by covering some basics related with the type of financial instruments that we will be using and why I have chosen them. I will also go through some basics related to the charts I will be showing you as well as how to properly interpret these graphs to get an idea about the historical performance of a given passive investment. We will also go into some of the key statistical metrics used in the basic interpretation of financial equity curves in order to compare investments in terms of returns, risk and risk-adjusted returns. I will also give you the code necessary to reproduce these graphs yourself (although this is not required to use the book's contents). If you're inclined to do so you should be able to reproduce everything shown within the book and perform any further analysis you might want to carry out. We will mainly use the free statistical software R for this, although if you want to ignore this code feel free to do so.

Within the second chapter we will cover a very important concept – the corner stone of this book – which is the use of leverage. We will go into what leverage is, what types of leverage there are, what it usually means to use leverage and what the costs of the different ways to apply leverage are. We will also go into the risks of using leverage in investments and the manner in which leverage can play against you. I will also talk here about why leverage has such a bad reputation and why retail investors are generally told to "run away" from leveraged products and strategies as fast as possible and why this fear should not be present if leverage is well understood.

After this chapter we will then go into the use of passive income strategies that use leverage as an integral part of them. I will talk about relationships between different market instruments and how fundamental differences in correlations can dramatically reduce the risks inherent to leveraged strategies. We will also talk about the types of instruments that we will use to construct a well-balanced leveraged portfolio using the different types of leverage described in chapter 2 and we will show the risk and return characteristics of these portfolios. You will see how the picture changes completely from leverage causing great increases in risk to a picture where leverage allows us to do things that would otherwise be impossible to do. This chapter will clearly show you why these strategies require leverage and how its use both increases historical returns and decreases risks.

In the next chapter we will then go into ways to maximize the potential returns of our leveraged strategies using smarter ways to enter the market with new investment capital. We will talk about how to update an analysis of these passive portfolios and time market entries in a way that is mostly beneficial to the growth of your portfolio. You will learn how to update your analysis as often as you like to capture entry opportunities and maximize the growth potential of your investment with minimum time expenditure. It is also worth noting that it is not necessary to apply the strategies in this chapter to build your leveraged passive income portfolio but these are just smart ways in which you can further increase your long term returns without having to spend a ton of time. If however you want to be as hands-free as possible you can avoid applying this knowledge and just use the information given in the previous chapter to build your portfolio.

Within the last chapter we will do a summary of all the above in order to draw some clear conclusions that will again reiterate why leverage in the end can be a very useful tool that – in the right hands – can lead to a large increase in profit and yes – a decrease in risk relative to a stock index – in a passive investment portfolio. I will also go into some further detail about how you can expand on the knowledge given in this book and start building and evaluating your own leveraged passive investment strategies. By this point you should be able to build and track your leveraged passive income portfolio and reap the rewards of this great investment approach.

Exchange Traded Funds

The financial instruments that we will use to build our investment portfolios are called Exchange Traded Funds (ETFs). These work like stocks in many ways, meaning that you can buy or sell them on stock exchanges and they pay dividends. They have big advantages over other instruments in that they allow us to gain specific exposure to some particular type of investment that would otherwise be hard to achieve.

Say for example you want to follow the market. When we say this we imply that you want your investment performance to resemble what financial people consider "investment benchmarks" like the S&P 500 (top 500 companies per Standard & Poors judgment) or something like the Dow industrial index (30 large publicly traded companies representing broad industrial sectors in the economy). If you wanted to follow the Dow you would then need to purchase stocks for these 30 companies and pay commissions on all those trades, plus the minimum required capital would be the sum of the individual stock prices of all those companies plus the commissions. We can already see that the cost would be large as would the account balance necessary to execute this strategy. Furthermore, selling this position would imply selling at least shares for 30 different companies, another added complication.

Alternatively we might just buy an ETF called DIA which tracks the Dow Jones for us. We pay around 244 dollars per share (its current price in 2018) and a single trade commission and we are getting the same results as if we were buying those 30 stocks. Sure, we pay a management fee to the ETF provider, which is a 0.17% that comes from the dividend of the ETF – which is paid every month in this case – and we have the comfort of having done a single market operation, with a very modest minimum investment. If we want to exit we sell that stock and pay the commission and that's it. We didn't have to buy stocks from 30 companies, nor pay 30 commissions. While we own DIA if the Dow went up 0.2% for example, we would get close to 0.2% up and if it went down by 0.2% we would also lose close to 0.2%. The ETF's result will generally be extremely close to the index, the difference – which is called the tracking error – is usually extremely low for these very highly liquid, market index ETF instruments.

In the same way in which we can buy an ETF to mimic the Dow we can buy different ETFs to mimic different indexes or other types of investments. For example we might buy the SPY ETF if we want to follow the S&P500 – without having to buy shares from 500 companies – or we might buy TLT to get exposure to 20+ year US treasury bonds. There are thousands of different ETF offerings and they are the ideal trading instruments to easily build passive investment portfolios with very high diversification without needing to do hundreds of financial transactions.

Another advantage of the ETFs is the fact that they are treated mostly like stocks, which allows us to use leverage. Although this is a concept that we will go into great detail in the next chapter it is worth noting that when using financial instruments like mutual funds leverage cannot be used with the same freedom and mutual funds that do include leverage are heavily restricted by law to a small amount of it that would hinder the execution of many of the strategies put forward in this book. Mutual funds are also more costly and provide less flexibility to investors, which we require for the portfolio construction methods I will explain later on. Although mutual funds can certainly have some advantages for some investment strategies, they do not work very well for the portfolios I will be covering.

Looking at charts

One of the most important tools we will be using through this book is historical performance, mostly in the form of historical equity curves. These are important as they can tell us how investments have behaved in the past and can tell us a lot about what scenarios we might expect in the future. Although past performance never guarantees future results, the past – especially for fixed passive portfolios – does provide important insights into the realm of potential outcomes. It is therefore critical for you to understand how to interpret these charts, especially in the format that we will be using through this book.

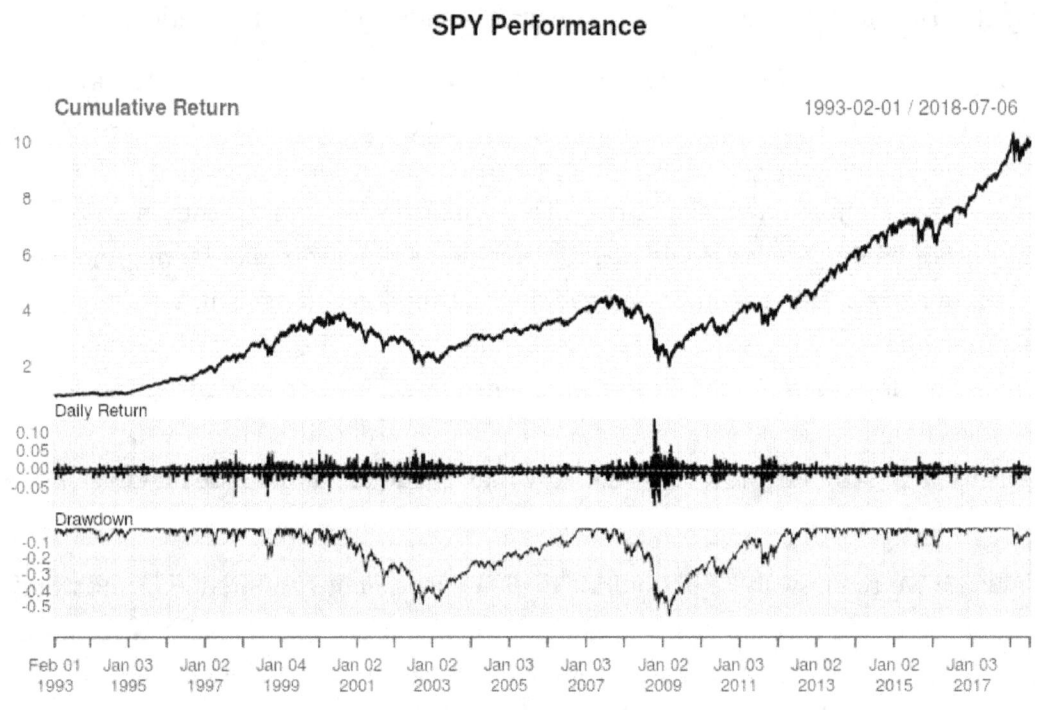

Figure 1: Historical Performance of the SPY ETF since 1993

In the figure above you can see an example of the historical performance charts we will be using. These charts are drawn using the PerformanceAnalytics package in R with free end-of-day data obtained from Yahoo financial using the quantmod package. We use the adjusted close price to build these graphs as the adjusted close price takes into account things like dividends and splits, greatly simplifying our view of historical performance beyond simply closing prices (which would lead us to wrong conclusions unless we explicitly accounted for dividends and splits ourselves).

In this graph the x-axis represents time – from 1993 to 2018 – while the y-axis on the top most graph represents the cumulative return of the ETF. This means that if we had bought the SPY ETF in 1993 we would have made around 10 times our money by 2018.

The graph in the middle represents the daily returns of the ETF and we can use it to gauge how volatility has increased or decreased as the years have passed. For example we can see that this band was much broader during the end of the 90s (dot com bubble) and during the financial crash in 2008-2009. This means that swings were larger – both towards the up and downsides – meaning that the ETF was a lot more nerve-wrecking during these times.

The last portion – which is commonly called an underwater plot – shows us the temporary losses the ETF has suffered through time. When this line dips we get an idea of how much drawdown or loss – as a fraction of equity – this ETF has had through time from its highest point up to before that moment. When it sits at zero it basically tells us that the ETF is making new highs. Looking at this underwater plot we can clearly see that the SPY ETF went into a drawdown of more than 40% (-0.4) during the dotcom bubble and more than 50% (-0.5) during the 2008 financial crisis while it has basically had no big drawdowns from 2009 to 2018, making new all-time highs consistently from 2013.

This underwater plots will be very important for our analysis as these plots give as a good idea about the historical risk of the investments we are taking on. We always want to both increase our returns and decrease our risks and we will therefore keep a watchful eye on these plots the entire time in order to gauge the losses of our passive investment portfolios and their historical behavior under stressful market conditions. Sometimes these plots will contain more than a single curve, allowing us to easily compare different investment methodologies.

Comparing different investment portfolios

Through this book we will go into many different investment portfolios in order to see which one might be better than another. Although the above curves will play a key role in helping us determine which one is the best choice we can also use statistical metrics to help us make this decision. These metrics are simple numbers that measure different properties of the equity curves and allow us to draw simple one-dimensional comparisons between them. There are potentially hundreds of statistical measurements we could make in order to assess historical portfolio performance but we will focus on a few simple ones in order to keep the analysis as straightforward and easy to understand as possible.

The first metric we will use will be the average annualized return (AAR) which is a simple measurement of the average return per year of a given investment as a fraction of its value at the beginning of each year. It can be calculated via the Return.annualized function in the PerformanceAnalytics package in R. As an example the SPY has had an AAR of 0.095 from 1993, meaning that – on average – it has returned 9.5% since then. The AAR is useful for several things, among them simple approximations like the "Rule of 72" which says that you can approximate the time needed to double your money based on a given AAR by dividing 72 by this value. In the case of the SPY this would give us a time of doubling of 72/9.5 or doubling our money around every 7.5 years. The AAR will be our main mechanism to measure returns as it's an intuitive and useful metric to gauge returns at a time scale that is most intuitive to us.

To measure risk we will use a metric called the maximum drawdown which measures the largest peak to valley distance in an equity curve as a fraction of the peak. It can be calculated using the maxDrawdown function in the PerformanceAnalytics package. In the case of the SPY example we have been looking at, the maximum drawdown value is 0.55, meaning that this investment at some point reached a loss of 55%. As illustrated in the graphs showed before, this happened during the 2008 financial crisis. Contrary to the AAR the maximum drawdown is not an average statistic but an extreme statistic since when talking about risk we are usually not interested in the average risk we will be facing but in the most extreme risk that has appeared.

Finally to get a sense of the risk adjusted return of the series we will be using the Sharpe ratio statistic – calculated via the SharpeRatio.annualized function in PerformanceAnalytics – which will give us an idea about the risk-adjusted return performance of a given investment. The Sharpe ratio is nothing but the mean daily return divided by the standard deviation of returns and allows us to get a sense of whether one investment has better risk per return or a better "bang for your buck" compared to another one. The SPY example before has an annualized Sharpe ratio value of 0.52, which means that the mean return is around half of the average volatility. The values for this statistic make little sense on their own and are better used to compare different investments on even ground.

It is also worth noting that we must always make comparisons of these statistics between investments across the same time periods. Meaning that if one investment has data from 1993 and another only from 1998 we cannot compare one set of statistics from 1993-2018 and another from 1998-2018 but we must either only use data from 1998-2018 for the first investment or find a way to expand our data for the second investment all the way back to 1993.

	DIA (from 1998)	SPY (from 1998)	SPY (from 1993)
AAR	8.02%	7.11%	9.53%
Max Drawdown	51.80%	55.18%	55.18%
Sharpe Ratio	0.43	0.36	0.52

Table 1: Comparison between the SPY and DIA ETFs showing the SPY statistics from 1998 or 1993

The table above shows an example comparing statistics between the SPY and DIA ETFs. When comparing the DIA ETF – which only has data from 1998 – with the SPY we can see that a comparison with the SPY ETF statistics from 1993 would make the SPY appear to be the better investment – on unfair grounds – while if we compare them apples-to-apples – both from 1998 to present – we see that the DIA actually has a better Sharpe Ratio and return compared with the SPY across this same period.

It is also important to note that this comparison window needs to be large enough in order to be useful, as there needs to be enough time for the equity curves to go through several different market cycles. A comparison using just a few years of data will be irrelevant as the evolution of the market during this time would not significantly represent a broad enough set of market conditions. In general the more data the better but at the very least we want to have a few market up and down turns within our curves to obtain more solid statistical measurements that would have a higher chance to properly build a set of future expectations. In some cases we might even use proxies – market instruments that are highly similar to the ones we're using but have longer historical data – to extend our historical expectations further back in time, allowing us to get a clearer picture of how things behaved under more varied market conditions. In some cases we will do this using mutual funds that are highly correlated with the ETFs we will be studying, not because we would be trading them in reality, but because we can use them as fair proxies to get a glimpse of performance at a time when the ETFs we're actually using just didn't exist. This will allow us to expand simulations further into the past, allowing us to gauge an investment strategy from – for example – 1985 instead of limiting us to only looking at it from say 2012.

A note about portfolio allocations and re-balancing

All the portfolios shown in this book assume that your investment is always distributed as indicated in terms of equity. For example if a portfolio invests 50% in SPY and 50% in TLT it assumes that everyday the amount of money in your portfolio will be half in SPY and half in TLT. This is done in order to eliminate any starting point dependency issues, to ensure that performance metrics are independent of when you would start investing.

Achieving a perfect allocation is easy when you start your investment – as you can simply buy 50% of your money in SPY shares and 50% in TLT shares for example – but this number will start to deviate as one investment makes or loses more money than the other. It might be that you start with a 25,000 USD investment that is 12,500 USD in TLT and 12,500 in SPY but after a year you might find yourself with 15,000 USD in TLT and 18,000 in SPY, which would change your allocation to 54.54% SPY and 45.46% TLT.

This effect is not likely to be important in the short term but it can accumulate to large proportions in the longer term, especially after a couple of years have passed. For this reason I would advice re-balancing your portfolio at least once a year in order to ensure that your allocation matches what you intend without incurring into any significant long term trading costs. If you have access to lower trading costs or you must comply with a given minimum number of transactions with your broker then more frequent re-balancing can be done. However it is worth noting that you shouldn't re-balance too frequently as this will make you incur significant additional costs with no straightforward benefit. At most I would advice re-balancing to be done on a bimonthly basis. You can also take advantage of money additions to your investment to rebalance your portfolio, this is what I generally do in order to keep my portfolio well balanced through time.

The R code appendix

This book contains an appendix in which I have placed all the R code that is necessary to reproduce all the figures within it. Within this code you will be able to see the way in which I have calculated out all the statistics and simulations for the portfolios showed through this book. I encourage you to double check my work and make sure to contact me if you notice any mistakes so that I can promptly fix them in future editions. Although I have made my best effort to double-check all the math and have passed the code through a few colleagues as well, I cannot provide absolute assurance that no mistakes have escaped my review process.

Leverage

Introduction to leverage

When I started my investment career in the summer of 2007 – at the ripe age of 21 – I had a desire to amass large amounts of profit in the shortest amount of time with little care for risk. My first contact with the markets came in the form of a Forex trading account, as a few friends told me that Forex trading was the quickest way to riches and glory. I ordered a couple of trading books and put 400 USD I had made flipping burgers into that account.

In the Forex market – which is the market where global currencies are exchanged – movements tend to be really small so it is typical for traders in this area to use leverage to increase the magnitude of their profits and losses. When you "use leverage" you borrow money from someone in order to use a market position that is larger than the amount of money you really have. In this way if you use 1:10 leverage it means that you would be able to trade with 100 USD even if you only have 10 USD. This means that you can turn a 0.1% move – up or down – into a 1% move. This also means that you can lose all your money with only a 10% move instead of a 100% move against you.

The leverage values available in Forex are much larger than those available in the stock market and I was quick to realize how risky this can be. During the first two weeks of trading the market I took my account from 400 USD to almost 1600 USD and then down to zero. Leverage had showed me how it could both amplify my returns and my losses and how trying to naively beat the market without a solid statistical edge was nothing but an exercise in futility.

In essence leverage is an amplifier for your money, it amplifies both your profit and your losses and it is therefore neither good nor bad on its own. If you use it irresponsibly – as I did when I started trading Forex – you can make it a complete disaster for your finances but used responsibly, as I will show you in the following chapters of this book, it can mean the difference between normal and extraordinary returns for your passive investment portfolios.

Warren Buffet has a very famous quote about leverage in which he says that if you're smart you don't need leverage and if you aren't smart you shouldn't use it. In reality if you are smart and you have time you absolutely don't need leverage to arrive at great returns – what we discussed in the first chapter of this book – but given a lack of time and a desire to invest in a smarter manner, leverage can play a key role in helping us boost our investment portfolios while helping us reduce risk compared with more traditional options like a plain index tracking ETF like DIA or SPY.

Types of leverage

There are two different ways in which leverage can normally be accomplished in a retail trading account. The first is called "trading on margin" which means you borrow money from your broker – at an interest – in order to use it for trading. Most brokers will allow you to trade with up to around 1:2 leverage which means you can borrow one dollar for every dollar you have in your account. The most important variable here to consider is the interest you pay on this borrowed margin, which will depend on both your broker and the size of your trading account. For a typical broker like Interactive Brokers the annual interest on margin on a USD account with less than 100,000 USD is 3.41%. This means that if we have a 10,000 account and we trade with an additional 5,000 – a 1.5 leverage – we will be paying 3.41% of those 5,000 – the amount we borrowed – per year. In practice this implies an annual start with a 170.5 USD loss, meaning we start each year having to make at least 1.70% just to break even. You can start to see here why considering the cost of interest on margin is so important, since it would be very easy for a leveraged strategy to lose all of its appeal due to the penalty caused by the interest we need to pay.

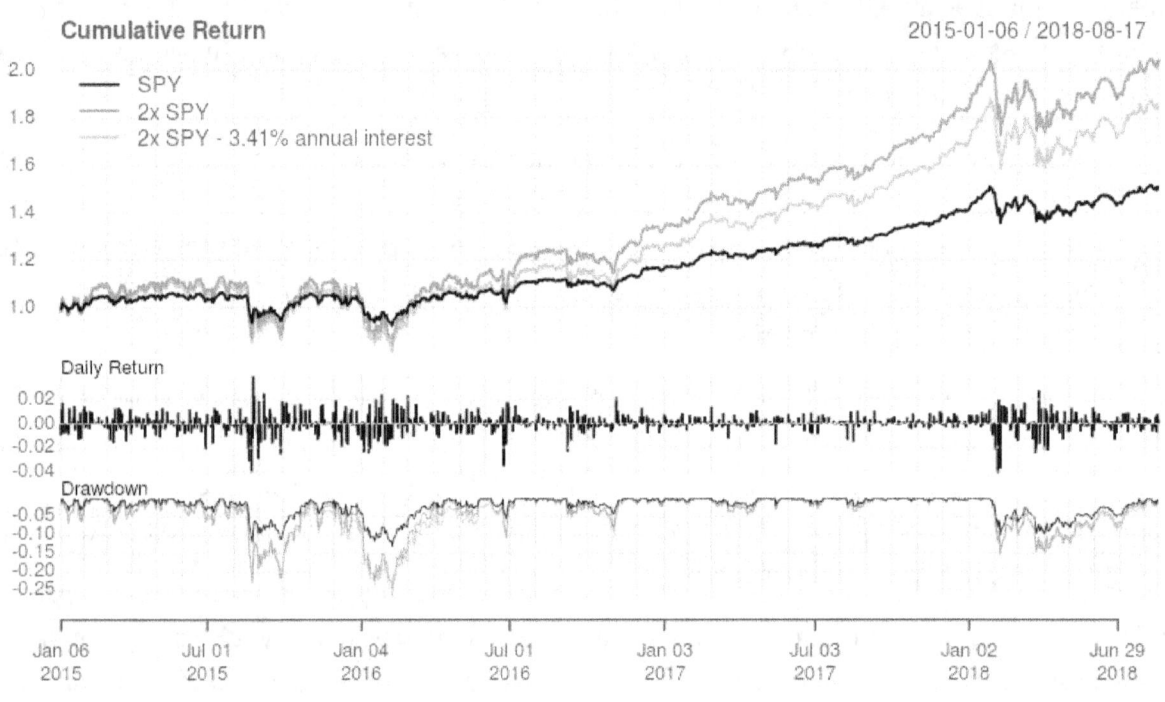

Figure 2: Comparison between unleveraged and leveraged SPY positions without rebalancing with and without costs.

The interest on margin is the biggest disadvantage of the "trading on margin" approach to leverage since the cost is generally very high for average retail trading accounts. Even worse, many retail brokers have margin costs that are even higher than this, making margin trading completely unfeasible since you often need to pay 5-8% of interest on margin, which implies an even worse handicap to your trading returns. Whenever you're considering using margin to leverage your account you should seriously consider whether this is worth it given the interest rate charged by your broker. Another important point is that this interest on margin also varies with the reference interest rate for your deposit currency. If your account is denominated in USD the interest you pay on margin will increase every time the federal reserve increases their reference interest rate. It is therefore necessary to recalculate whether a margin based leveraged approach is worth it every time interest rates vary considerably.

In Figure 2 you can see a comparison from 2015 of trading the SPY, the SPY with an initial 2x leverage without any interest and the SPY using an initial 2x leverage paying the interest cost that would be demanded by a broker for trading this ETF on margin. The average annualized results for the three outcomes are 11.90%, 21.58% and 18.48%. We can see that ignoring the interest would fool us into thinking this historical period would have given us a 21.58% annualized return while in reality the return would have only been around 18.48%. The interest paid to the broker had a huge impact on our final returns, in this case doubling our initial risk – with the 2x leverage – didn't pay off very well in terms of returns since our final result was only around 1.54 times that of the SPY due to the incurred trading costs.

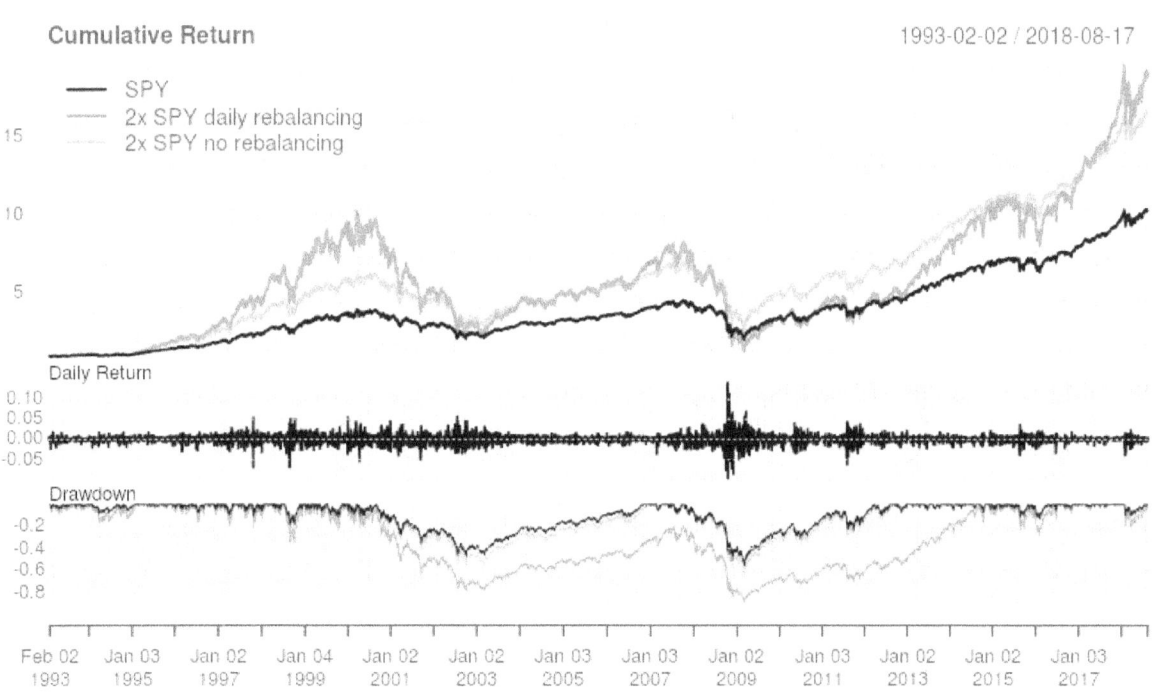

Figure 3: Effect of daily rebalancing on leveraged SPY positions (including 3.41% annual interest over borrowed margin)

It is also worth noting that leveraged trading approaches using margin are usually not adjusted very frequently – especially if we're talking about passive investments – meaning that your leverage in dollar terms will be constant as a function of time and won't be adjusted as your balance grows (as this would imply paying commissions to buy/sell shares to exactly reflect 2x your current capital level at every point in time). This approach effectively dilutes your leverage as a function of time if your money grows, meaning that although you started borrowing 1 dollar for every dollar you had, in the end you were only borrowing 0.4 dollars for every dollar you had. As shown in Figure 3 the lack of rebalancing can have big effects in terms of how your equity curve will behave. This is because there is a big difference between starting with 2x the shares of SPY, keeping them as a function of time paying interest on their initial cost, and effectively changing your number of shares daily such that your exposure represents 2x of your current balance every day. Daily rebalancing leads to reproducing 2x the daily returns of the SPY minus interest while not rebalancing implies that the magnitude of your interest payments will indeed decay as a function of time as they will become smaller and smaller. This also means that how you do will depend heavily on when you bought those initial 2x shares, making strategies that are not rebalanced much more entry dependent.

Although the leveraged strategy without rebalancing in Figure 3 looks much better in terms of risk-adjusted returns – as we risked less to make almost the same amount of money in the end – it is only so because of the starting point. A leveraged strategy without leverage rebalancing can look better or worse than a daily rebalanced strategy depending on when exactly you started, since your leverage decays as a function of time from this starting point. There is a large unpredictability related with the starting point that doesn't exist with daily rebalancing.

The big advantage of "trading on margin" is the freedom that it gives you. When you trade with margin there is almost no limit to the instruments you can buy with this borrowed money as you can practically buy all instruments you could buy with your normal money. There are some exceptions to this – like mutual funds – but the freedom you have with margin trading is unprecedented compared with the other approach we will be discussing. Another key aspect is that you can use as little or as much leverage – up to your maximum – as you want, while with the approach I will be explaining next you are heavily constrained in this regard.

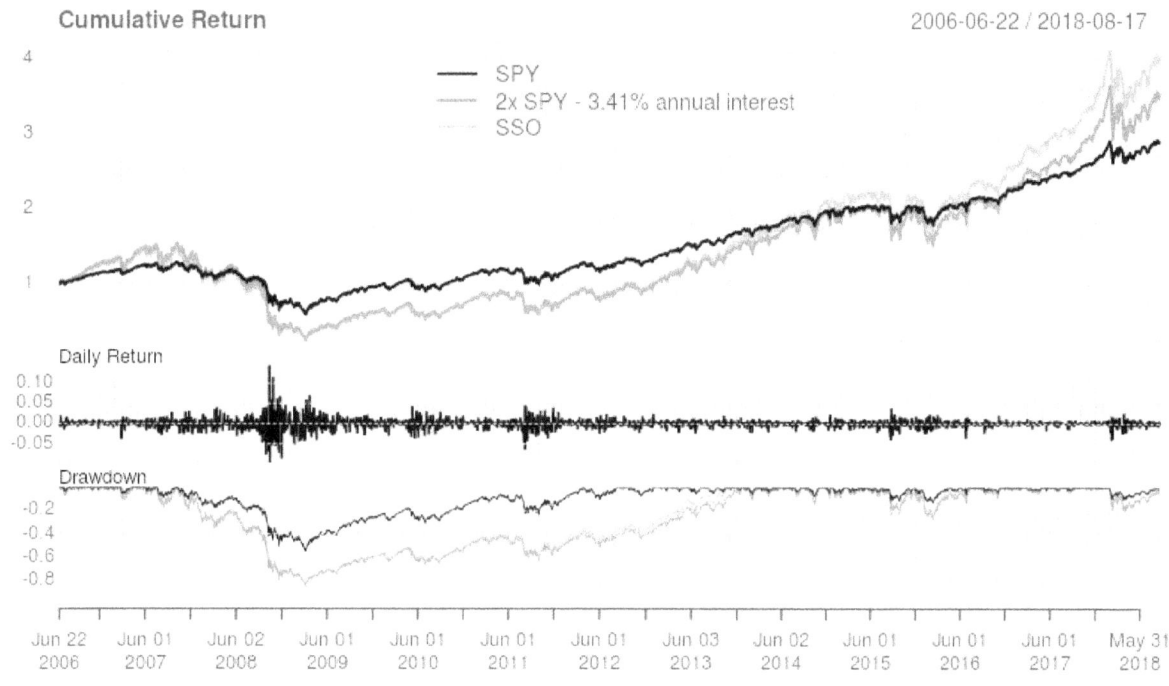

Figure 4: Comparison between an implied leverage position using SSO and a 2x margin position paying interest and doing daily rebalancing

The second approach to leverage is what I will call "implicit leverage", this is when you don't borrow any money yourself but you buy a market traded ETF where this leverage is already included in what the ETF tracks. Let's say for example that you want to trade the SPY ETF with a 1:2 leverage, there is an ETF product called SSO which allows you to do exactly that. In leveraged ETF products you pay the "borrowing cost" as a more expensive management fee in the ETF – so your dividends in SSO will be lower than 2x that of the SPY – with the advantage that your leverage is automatically kept at 2x everyday, meaning you never need to worry about rebalancing since the ETF managers ensure that you will always get as close as possible to the promised leverage multiplier. This means that you are much less entry dependent than with a margin approach that doesn't go through rebalancing.

In terms of trading costs the implicit leverage strategy will beat the margin leveraged strategy every time mainly due to the costs involved in constant rebalancing of the margin strategy and the interests we need to pay. Figure 4 shows that just the interest alone is enough to make SSO a better strategy than a daily rebalanced margin leveraged strategy, even if we didn't have to pay any trading costs for the rebalancing.

Leverage and compounding

The consequences of using leverage are often heavily misunderstood, especially if daily rebalancing is involved. This is a common reason why many run away from using leverage in their trading. Most people talk about things like "beta decay" or "volatility decay" when using leverage, alluding to how you end up with something that is different from the X multiplier you would intuitively expect from using a certain amplification on your capital (like what happens when you simply start with 2x the number of shares in a margin based approach and never rebalance). This comes from problems in understanding what is being amplified and the consequences that this has.

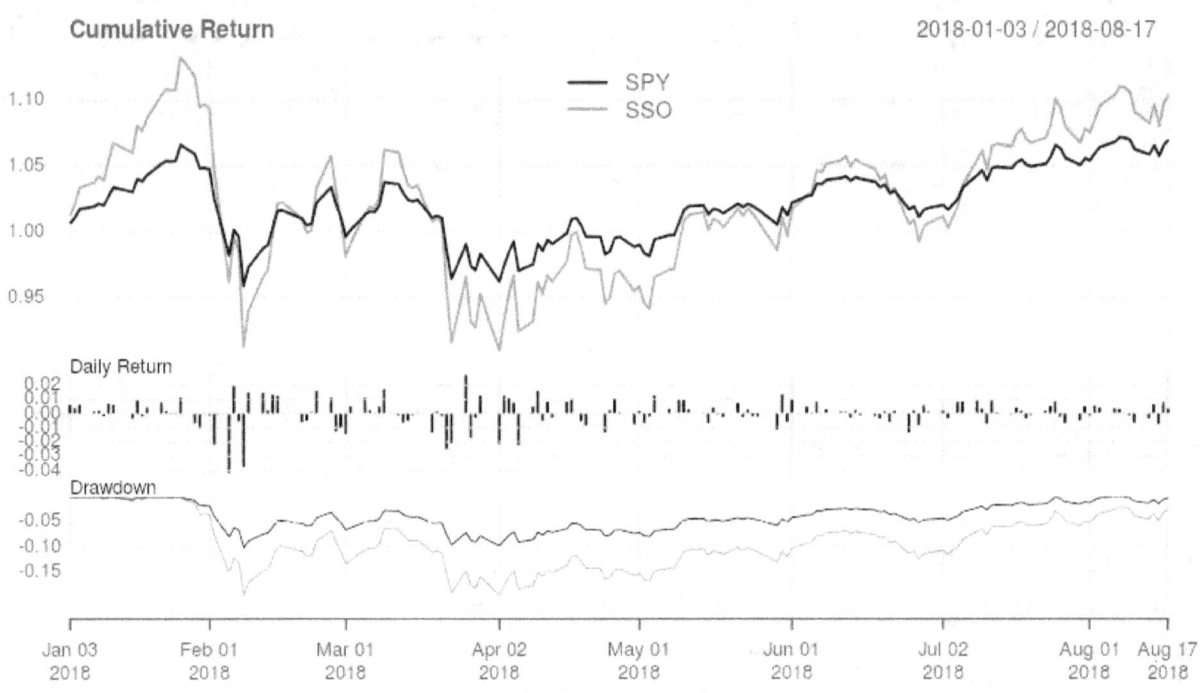

Figure 5: Comparison between SSO - which is 2x SPY - and SPY performance

It's important to understand that we are amplifying the daily returns on our money, and not the end-result, when we use leverage and rebalance daily. This is especially important with the implied leverage strategies, where daily rebalancing is always being done. So the fact that you use 1:2 leverage does not mean that you will end up with the equivalent of having owned 2x the amount of shares in the end or that you will be making 2 times more per year, it means that your daily returns will be doubled, an effect that can lead to some surprising results.

In Figure 5 you can see a comparison between a normal position on the SPY and an SSO position – which tracks 2x SPY – for the year 2018 up to August 17th. In the end the returns of the 2x position are not 2x those of the normal position (6.66% Vs 4.91%), this is a consequence of amplifying the daily returns and paying borrowing expenses which makes the ending math result more complicated than what you would intuitively expect. The maximum loss for the SSO is also 19.76% while that of the normal position is 10.10%. In the end we both had a lower maximum drawdown and final return than 2x with the leverage position, a result that can seem misleading.

You can also see that sometimes within the graph the lines do not cross the 1.0 line at the same time, meaning that in some cases we can be making money for the year on an unleveraged position and losing money on a leveraged position or vice versa. Imagine you lost 5% on a single trading day on the normal position, this means you would need to make 5.26% to recover – because you now have less money so need to make a larger return to recover your original capital – while on a 2x position that loss of 5% would be turned to 10% and you would need 11.1% to recover. If the following day we made 5.1% this would take our unleveraged position to 99.84% of the original capital while our leveraged position will be at 100.08%. Note that the case can easily be the opposite due to the cost of leverage – which is very important as we saw before – but my point is that the math of compounding makes differences between the outcomes of leveraged and unleveraged positions relatively difficult to intuitively predict.

Because of all the above you shouldn't rely on intuition in order to draw conclusions about the expected performance and risks of leveraged strategies but you should always carry out simulations of the passive portfolios adequately taking into account the costs – if any – inherent to the leveraged strategy. All the above does not constitute a reason not to use leverage but it does point out the fact that the effects of using leverage are by no means trivial to understand and approaches to leverage should be well thought out. In this book I have taken care to always include interests on margin or use adjusted close data for leveraged ETF instruments, ensuring that the return graphs and statistics shown reasonably reflect the results that would have been obtained historically while following these approaches.

The risks of using leverage

Many of you might have noticed the 80%+ drawdowns present in Figures 3 and 4 in the past sections. This is without a doubt the reason why most money managers and investors tell people to run away from leveraged ETF products and margin trading and to completely avoid using any of these tools as long term investment strategies. This certainly sounds reasonable considering the huge risk that a person would put their money at if they followed a simple 2x leveraged index investing strategy. The fact that the historical worst case during the past 20+ years has put 2x positions close to a complete account loss highlights the fact that leveraged products should not be used lightly.

Moreover it is important to consider that there are even more highly leveraged ETF offerings out there with 3x and even 4x index products that can seriously jeopardize the survival of a person's trading account, even under medium term scenarios. I am no stranger to these risks and the high risk of ruin inherent to long term investments using solely these trading vehicles but I want you to rest assured that my investment strategies are not simply leveraged index investments. The strategies we will be discussing rely on strong market relationships in order to ease the risk inherent to the use of both margin or implied leverage.

I want to reiterate that naive leveraged approaches are indeed terribly risky and it is extremely important to do your homework when using leverage in trading, especially when doing leveraged passive investment strategies.

Within the next chapter we will be going into the actual portfolios we will be using to take advantage of leverage and you will see how we can both reduce risk and increase profitability relative to a simple unleveraged stock index ETF investment.

Leveraged Passive Income Portfolios

Introducing bond and stock portfolios

As we saw in the previous chapter the introduction of leverage in a simple indexed ETF greatly increases our level of risk. We saw how a simple SSO investment – which is 2x SPY – would have led us to a drawdown greater than 80% during the 2008 financial crisis. Naked exposure to a leveraged ETF of this nature might lead us to an almost total capital loss in the future. This is the reason why we need to use several different instruments to build a portfolio where the risks of different leveraged products can be compensated in order to achieve much better returns. We need investment products that are all expected to yield positive returns in the future but we need those returns to be as uncorrelated as possible in the short term.

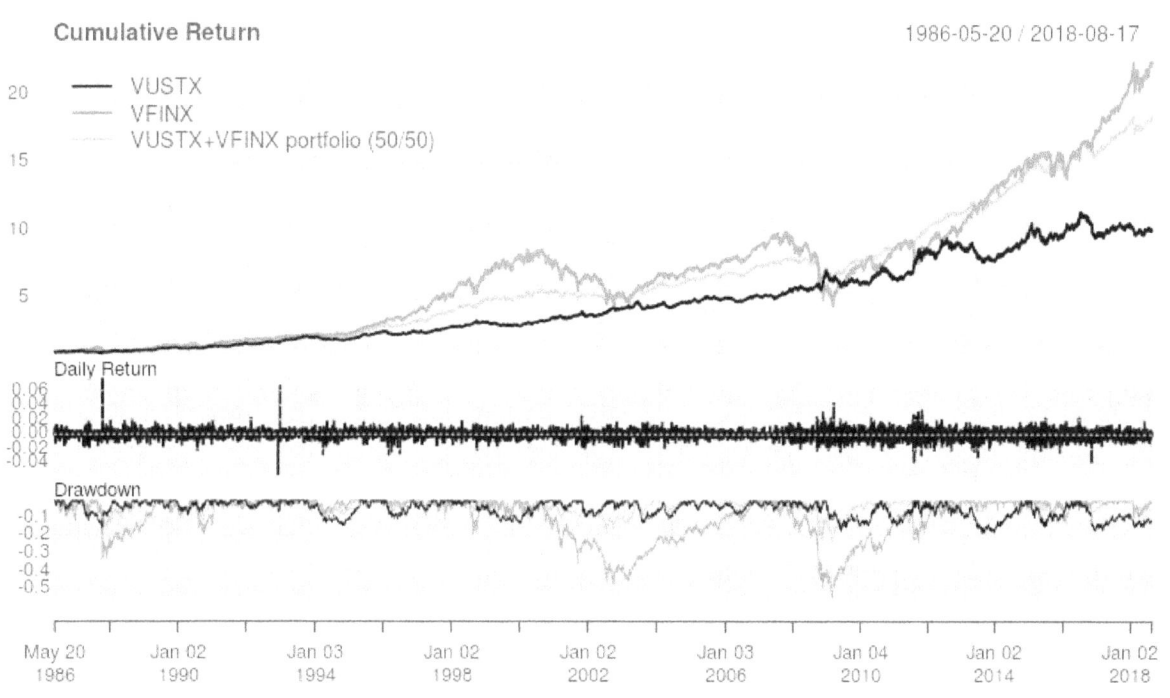

Figure 6: Comparison between VUSTX (tracking 20+ year US bonds), VFINX (tracking S&P 500) returns and a portfolio using a 50% allocation in each one.

The main two categories of products that we have available for investing are bonds and stocks, as these two product types are expected to yield positive returns. We will now discuss the relationships between these two types of investments and we will also see how we can use these instruments to create investment portfolios that use leverage and yield both increases in returns and decreases in risk relative to the performance of stock, bond or unleveraged stock/bond portfolios.

There are many types of bonds available in the market, going from very low risk to very high risk. Bonds that have low yields are generally associated with low risk while high yielding bonds are associated with higher risk investments. On the safe side we have things like US government and corporate bonds while on the higher risk side we have things like emerging market government bonds or small company bonds.

High yielding bonds are usually closely related to stocks, as investors put their money there for similar reasons (pursue of higher returns with a higher risk expectation), however, low yielding bonds are not strongly correlated with stock indexes because investors move their money there when the market is in trouble. You can observe this behavior in Figure 6 where we compare the VUSTX and VFINX mutual funds. The first of these funds tracks 20+ year US government bonds – a low risk bond investment – while the second tracks the S&P500. These serve as two long term proxies to their equivalent ETF counterparts, TLT and SPY, which only have data from 2002 and 1993 respectively.

	VUSTX	VFINX	50/50 Portfolio
AAR	7.39%	10.10%	9.41%
Max DD	18.42%	55.25%	24.88%
Sharpe	0.7	0.55	0.97

Table 2: Comparison between the statistics for VUSTX, VFINX and a 50/50 portfolio 1986-2018

It is especially important to look at behavior during moments of financial tension – 1987, 1999, 2008, etc – and see how US government bonds behave compared with stock returns, especially in the Drawdown plot. We can see that during these periods bonds have now gone into drawdown either at different times or proportionately much less compared to stocks. As a matter of fact during the beginning of most of these crisis bonds have gone up – while stocks have gone down sharply – meaning that US treasury bonds have consistently provided a good hedge against stocks during times of market turmoil. In fact the long term correlation between bonds and stocks is -0.15, showing us that bonds are loosely correlated with stocks although both instruments end up moving in the same direction (they both go up as a function of time).

From this it would be natural to consider a portfolio using both investments as a way to obtain better risk adjusted returns and we can indeed see in Table 2 how a 50/50 portfolio between these two mutual funds would achieve a return closer to that of the VFINX fund (9.41% vs 10.10%) with a drawdown that is less than half that of the VFINX fund. We have increased our returns so much relative to our risk that our Sharpe has increased to 0.97, which is much higher than the Sharpe we would get with either bonds or stocks. With this in mind it appears that the bond/stock portfolio is a clear winner over either the stock or the bond mutual fund proposition.

However there is a problem here, we have indeed reduced our returns relative to the stock investment, meaning that in the end we would finish with a cumulative return of 17 times our initial investment in our bond/stock portfolio instead of 21 times our initial investment in the stock mutual fund. This difference is significant and is attributed to the larger risk we took in the S&P500 tracking fund, which in the end led to higher absolute accumulated returns. However if we would be willing to take the same risks as in the stock market we can envision a leveraged hypothetical portfolio where we trade 2x the returns of the portfolio, paying interest to our broker to borrow the funds and ensuring our leverage is rebalanced daily. The results of doing this investment are shown in Figure 7 and show you how amazing the power of leverage can be.

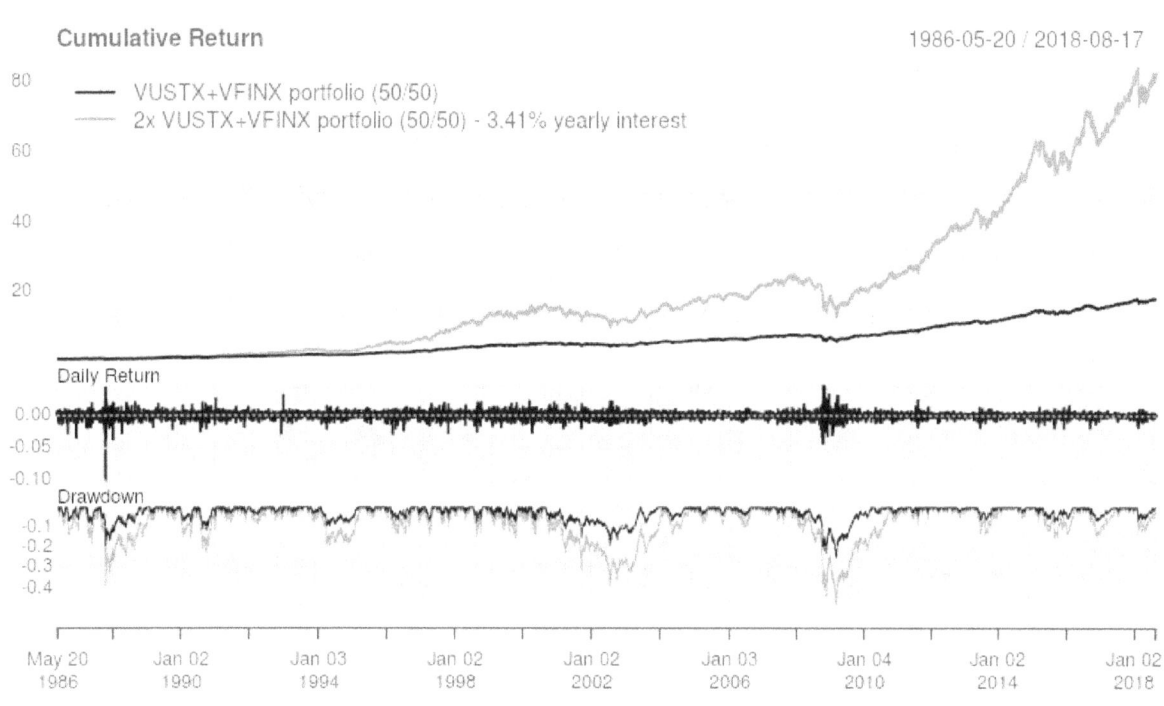

Figure 7: Comparison between leveraged and unleveraged VUSTX/VFINX portfolios

Our annualized returns have now increased from 9.41% to 14.6% while our maximum drawdown has also increased from 24.88% to 48.03%, we have indeed doubled our risk – which is still less than the loss we would have had in the VFINX fund – but we have increased our returns very substantially. Our accumulated returns from 1986 to present changed from 17 times our initial investment to 80 times our initial investment. Due to the power of compounding this 5.19% difference in returns expands into a

4.6 increase in absolute returns after 32 years. Here we have showed how if we're willing to accept the risks of the stock market we can actually perform much better if we use a leveraged version of the stock/bond portfolio. Our Sharpe has however decreased substantially – from 0.97 to 0.75 – owing to the interest we paid to maintain this daily 2x leverage through the 32 year period, although this Sharpe ratio is still much higher than that of the stock mutual fund investment.

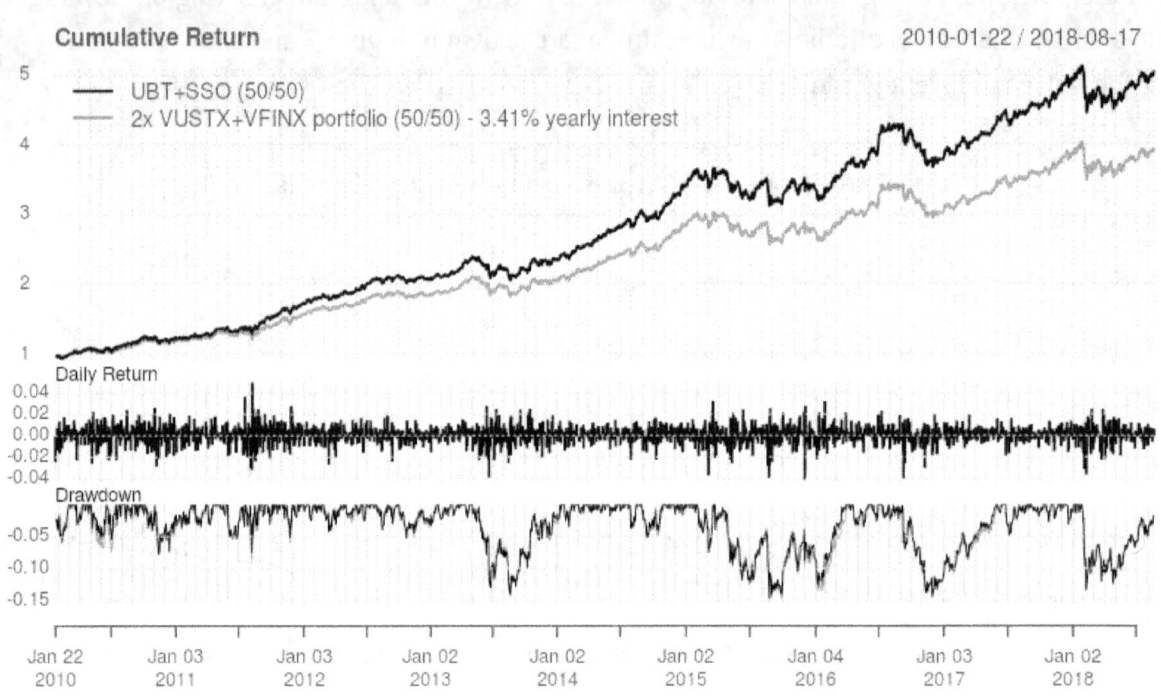

Figure 8: Comparison between a hypothetical VUSTX/VFINX leveraged portfolio and a UBT/SSO tradeable portfolio

It should be clear however that it is not realistic to perform a daily rebalanced 2x mutual fund investment but we need to do this with instruments that allow for the construction of an equivalent portfolio with hopefully no large rebalancing costs. We can indeed find this alternative in the SSO and UBT ETFs which represent 2x S&P500 and 2x 20+ year US government bonds. In this way we can construct an implicit leverage strategy that is equivalent to our mutual fund daily rebalanced long term analysis. Figure 8 shows you a comparison between our hypothetical mutual fund portfolio and the actually tradeable portfolio using UBT and SSO. You can see here that our UBT/SSO portfolio is indeed better performing due to the lower interest of an implicit leverage approach compared to a margin approach where we pay a significantly larger interest to our broker (which doesn't even count the cost we would need to pay in rebalancing!). The correlation between both approaches is 0.978, which shows that the UBT/SSO and leveraged VUSTX/VFINX approaches are equivalent, we have indeed constructed a realistically tradeable portfolio from our hypothetically leveraged mutual fund analysis. This portfolio already shows you how a leveraged bond/stock portfolio can indeed provide an increase in return and a decrease in risk relative to traditional unleveraged stock investments.

A note about bond/stock relationships

It is worth noting that the period from 1986 to present is a period of declining treasury bond yield rates, meaning that treasuries have systematically risen more in value thanks to a steady decrease in their overall yields. However it is important to note that the main driver behind the increase in value of bonds is not solely related with yields but with the actual payment of the bond yields, the issuing of new bonds and the desire of counter-parties to hold those bond relative to others. Indeed US bonds did increase in value under periods of increasing rates and increasing inflation. For example the PINCX fund – which is an aggregate US bond mutual fund that has data available since 1954[1] - shows this phenomena. Although for this fund the loss in 2008 is more pronounced that in a long term US government bond fund due to the inclusion of high yielding securities – like mortage bonds – you can see that bond performance was indeed very stable, even under earlier market conditions were interest rates were not declining. Other examples of funds with 40+ years of data showing this behavior are NTHEX, EKHBX, NCINX and SCSBX.

This demonstrates that rising rates are not a "death sentence" for bond funds although these environments might lead to much lower returns and even scenarios where returns do not overcome inflation. However we will indeed take into account the possibility of rising rates and inflation in the construction of our portfolios, reason why we will explore variants that try to protect us from these potential issues.

Choosing a stock ETF using capitalization

In the first section of this chapter we explored the construction of a simple bond/stock leveraged portfolio using 2x S&P 500 and 2x 20+ year government bond ETFs. We showed how an approach like this can indeed reduce volatility and increase returns relative to stock or bond investments, even under a 32 year historical evaluation. Now we can look at how we can actually change our stock ETF in order to have even better returns than those that are provided by an S&P 500 tracking ETF. We will focus on ways to choose a stock ETF that can maximize our returns in the future while we will try to minimize risks associated with selections based purely on hindsight (for example investing solely in technology stocks because they have performed so well in the past couple of decades).

The growth potential of a stock index is directly related with the growth potential of the individual companies within it and their failure probabilities. Depending on how we select the companies we can

---

1 You can view the entire history for PINCX here http://quotes.morningstar.com/chart/fund/chart?t=PINCX&region=USA&culture=en-US

have an index where companies are very stable – very low failure probability – but very unlikely to grow, for example if we choose only very large companies, or we can choose companies that have a lot of growth potential – smaller companies – with a larger probability to fail. There is however a "sweet spot" where growth potential increases substantially without large increases in risk, which is where we find middle capitalization companies, often refereed to as "mid caps". These are companies with between 2 and 10 billion dollars in market capitalization – so they are already stable by any measure – and we can indeed find many ETF products that allow us to buy mid cap based indexes. The MVV ETF provides us with 2x the daily returns of the S&P MidCap 400 Index, which is analogous to the S&P500 but for mid cap companies.

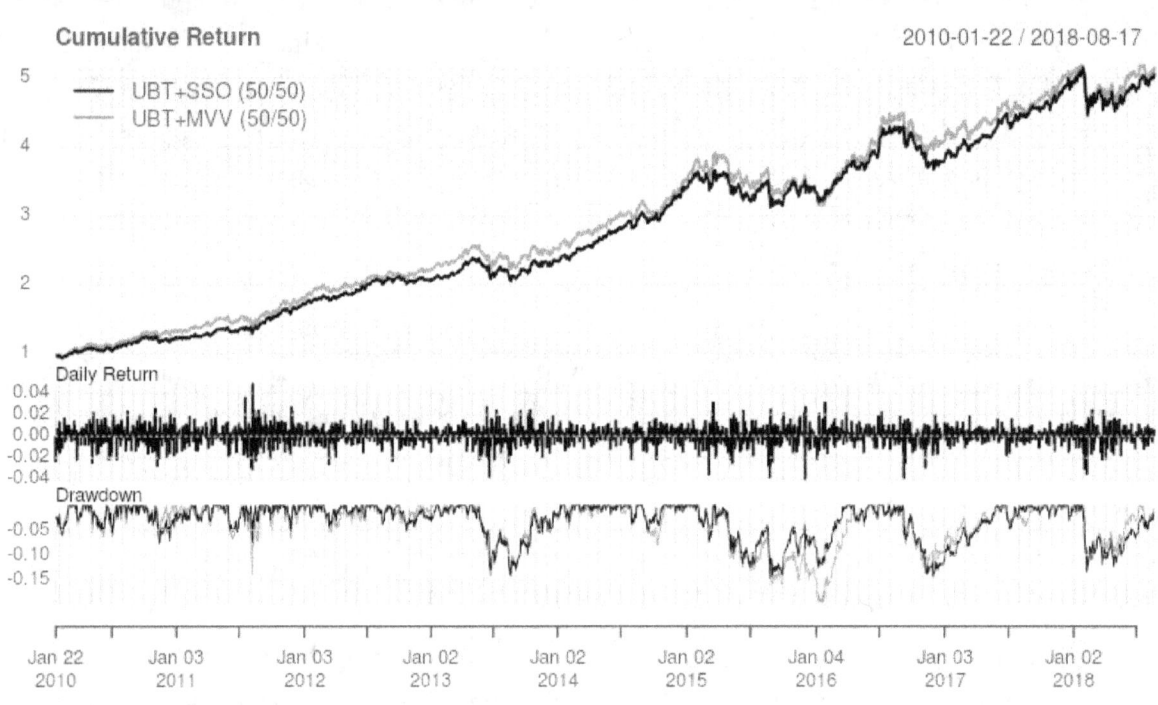

Figure 9: Comparison between UBT/SSO and UBT/MVV portfolios

Figure 9 shows you a return comparison of an MVV/UBT and an SSO/UBT portfolio. Although the MVV portfolio is slightly better performing it is hard to see why we would want to make a choice in favor of MVV as the maximum drawdown is indeed deeper and this does not seem to be properly compensated by a proportionately higher return. Since our scope here is very limited – only the past 8 years – we need to use an analogous long term mutual fund approach to make a proper judgment. The VIMSX mutual fund provides us with an opportunity to access much longer term mid cap data and we can use a leveraged VIMSX/VUSTX portfolio and compare it to our previous leveraged VFINX/VUSTX portfolio as a way to gauge the long term performance of both approaches.

Figure 10 shows you the comparison between these two daily rebalanced 2x approaches using mutual funds as proxies. Here we can clearly see how the mid cap approach is much more successful than the regular S&P500 approach. The maximum drawdown of the mid cap approach is indeed a bit higher – at 51.6% vs 48.03% - but the AAR has also increased significantly from 10.29% to 12.79%. For the price of a small increase in maximum drawdown we have achieved a very significant increase in the yearly growth rate which – as we saw in the previous sections – can lead to a very significant difference in long term returns. In this graph – which covers the period from 1998 to 2018 – the mid cap approach achieved a final return of 10.3x the capital while the S&P500 approach achieved 6.21x. We can also see that there are some periods – like 2000-2002 – when mid caps actually had less downside compared to the large capitalization companies present in the S&P500. This means that the mid cap approach actually ends up with a larger Sharpe ratio (0.62) compared with the S&P500 portfolio (0.55).

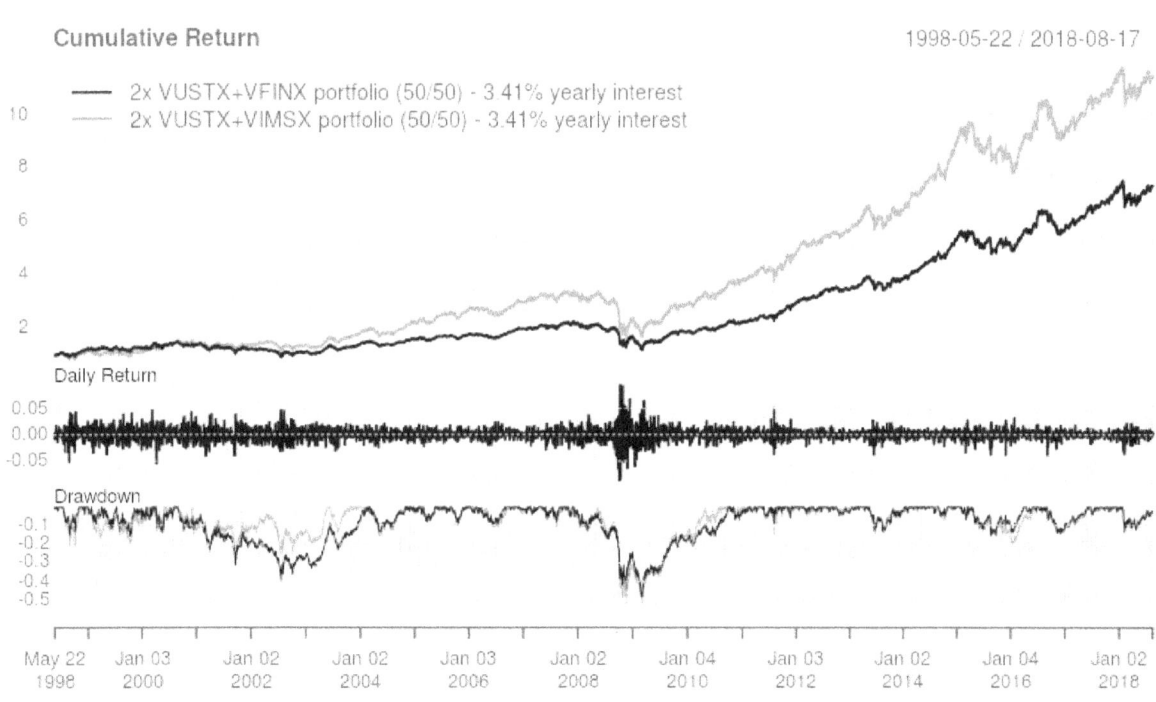

Figure 10: Comparison between VFINX and VIMSX leveraged portfolios

If you're willing to pay a small increase in risk for a substantial increase in potential returns selecting a mid cap ETF might be a very good choice. It is also worth noting that this relationship is very likely to continue going forward as it's clear that smaller stable companies have larger growth potential than very big companies that have a much harder time to expand the same amount in percentage points. This will remain the same in the future as new companies are created and some of the current mid cap companies eventually become larger cap companies.

You could also take this approach further with small capitalization companies (which are companies with 300 million to 2 billion in market capitalization). The S&P Small Cap 600 index helps us track a group of small capitalization companies in the same way as the mid cap index discussed before. However the problem with this is that we have no long term proxies for this index – since all mutual funds or ETFs that track it have track records shorter than 8 years – so it is risky to assume how such an investment would have behaved under past market turmoil. However if you're interested in trading using such an approach the SAA ETF provides you with a 2x leveraged representation of this index, the results of trading this against our UBT/SSO portfolio from 2010 are shown in Figure 11. During the recent past the SSA/UBT portfolio has performed better than the MVV/UBT approach with a similar overall risk, although it is fairly reasonable to expect the risk to be higher under more extreme conditions, like a 2008 crisis type event.

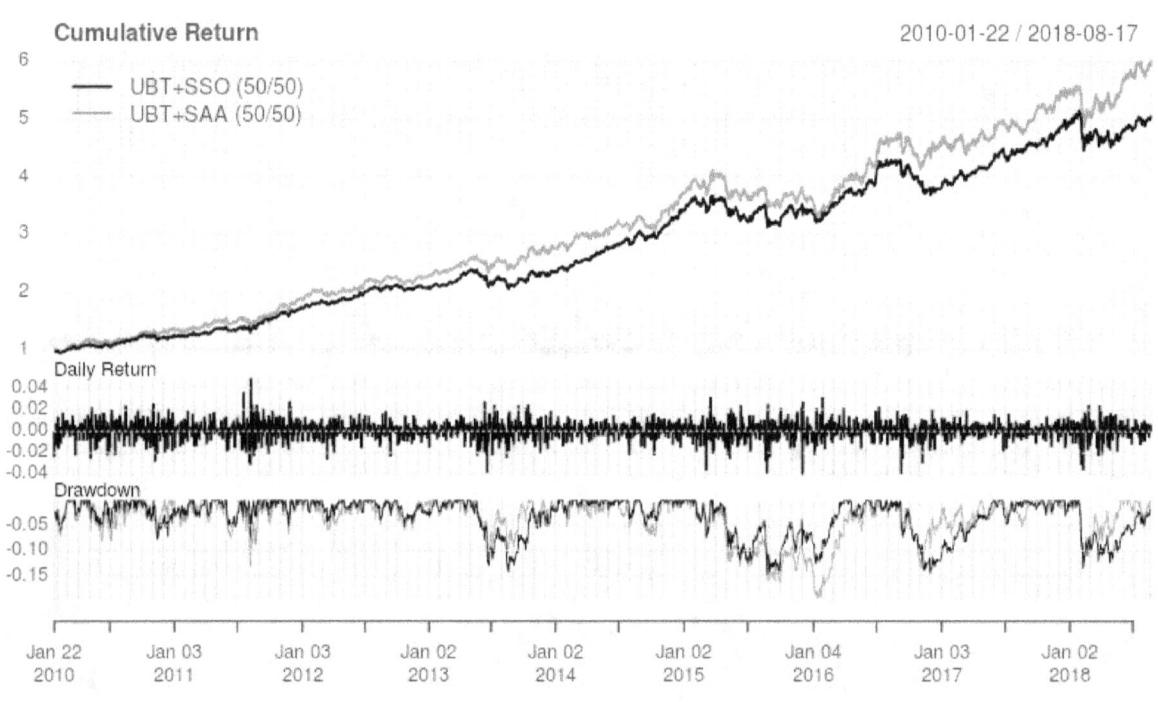

Figure 11: Comparison between SAA/UBT and SSO/UBT portfolio returns.

There are other approaches that can be used for the selection of a leveraged stock ETF – such as sectors, smart beta, etc – but all such approaches require you to take additional risks, for example expecting a particular sector to out-perform in the future. With a market capitalization approach our only assumption is that growth and risk are proportional to companies' size and potential, both of which are fundamentally likely to hold in the future.

Choosing a bond ETF

In the previous analysis we used UBT – which represents 2x 20+ year government bonds – as the bond components within our portfolios. This was done because of the low long term correlation between long term bonds and stocks, which we showed initially using the VUSTX and VFINX mutual funds. However we can also ask ourselves whether there is a better way to choose a bond component, especially if there is something we can do to make the portfolio much less volatile and potentially protect us from future increases in inflation and US government interest rates.

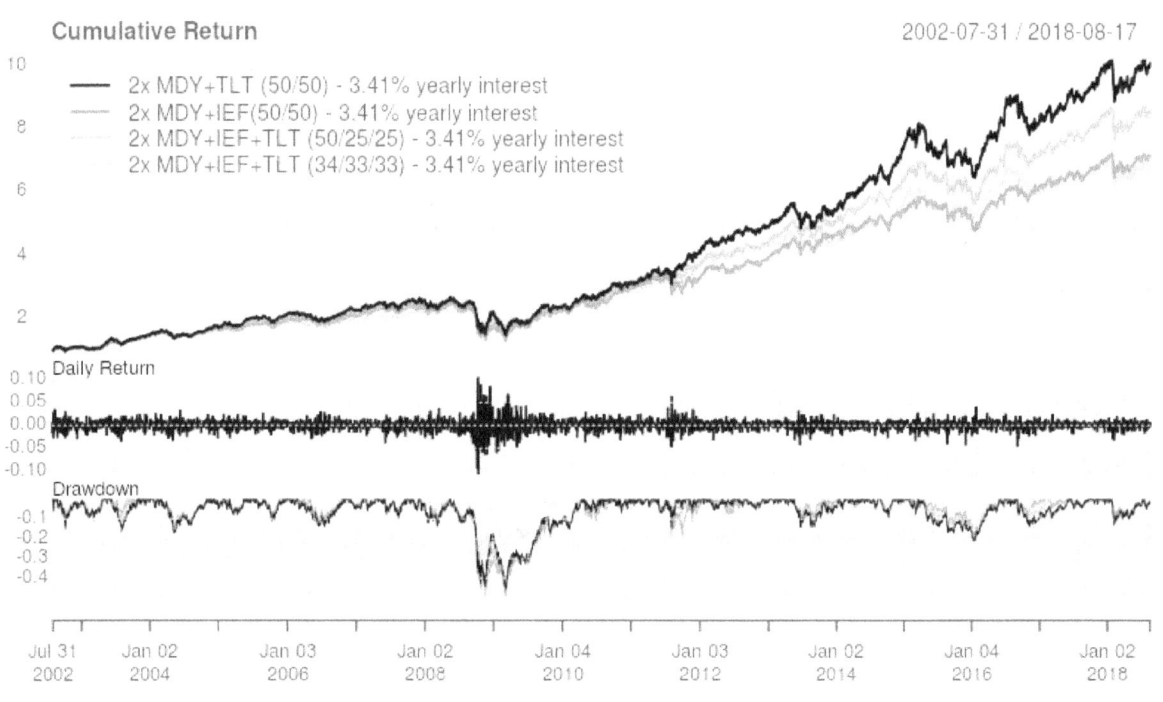

Figure 12: Results of different leveraged portfolios built using IEF, TLT and MDY

In order to protect us against future inflation and rising interest rates the easiest thing we can do is choose a bond component with a lower maturity date range. Instead of using 20+ year government bonds we can use a 7-10 year government bond ETF instead, which would be less sensitive to increases in interest rates in the future. To understand how this would work we will use the IEF, TLT and MDY ETFs – to get data back to 2002 – to build portfolios and we will look at their 2x daily rebalanced leveraged results paying interest on margin. We use IEF for 7-10 year government bonds, TLT for 20+ year government bonds and MDY for the S&P 400 mid cap index.

	MDY/TLT	MDY/IEF	MDY/IEF/TLT	MDY/IEF/TLT
Weights	50/50	50/50	50/25/25	34/33/33
AAR	15.26%%	12.90%	14.24%	12.61%
Max DD	45.54%	49.34%	47.32%	30.13%
Sharpe	0.77	0.66	0.73	0.84

Table 3: Statistical results for the different MDY/TLT/IEF 2x portfolios

The results from 2002 in Figure 12 and Table 3 show us that the biggest returns in this case belong to the MDY/TLT leveraged portfolio and become lower for all the alternative portfolios, with the lowest returns belonging to the MDY/IEF/TLT portfolio with equal allocation between the three instruments. However in this case the drawdown has fallen down to 30.13% vs close to 50% for all the rest of the portfolios. We can also see that introducing IEF instead of TLT does decrease both our Sharpe and our returns relative to TLT but introducing both IEF and TLT and equally distributing the portfolio weight between the three instruments achieves an added effect where the Sharpe is increased to the highest value in the table (0.84). Using a combination of MDY, IEF and TLT therefore achieves the best risk adjusted returns, although at the expense of some of the performance of a simpler MDY/TLT approach. We can translate this MDY/IEF/TLT approach to a portfolio using leveraged ETFs by using MVV/UBT/UST, where UST is an ETF seeking to reproduce 2x the daily returns of 7-10 year government bonds.

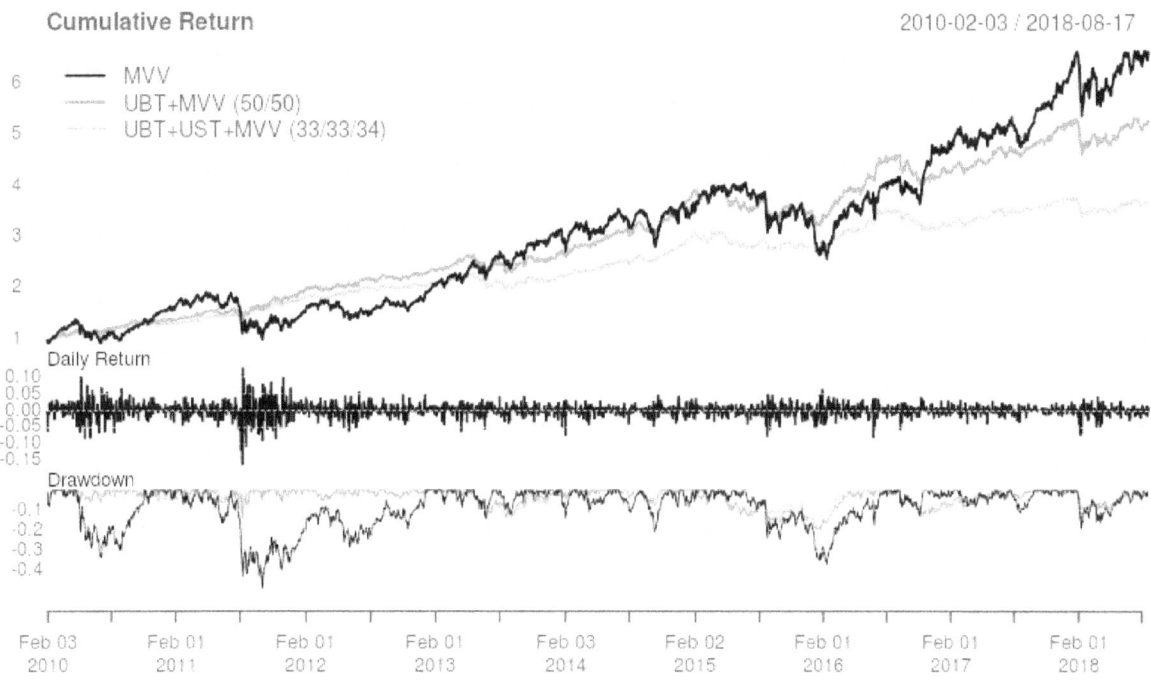

Figure 13: Results for UBT/UST/MVV portfolios

In Figure 13 we can see the results of using implicitly leveraged ETFs in order to trade these leveraged portfolios. During the recent past the MVV/UST/UBT portfolio has performed much worse than the MVV/UBT portfolio with returns of 16.39% and 21.25% respectively. The drawdown of the three instrument setup has indeed been lower (14.11% Vs 19.63%) and its Sharpe has not been higher (1.30 Vs 1.32) we could therefore say that under more recent conditions it has paid to avoid using this hedge but it is worth considering that a mixed MVV/UST/UBT approach might offer significant protections in a rising interest rate environment against a portfolio like MVV/UST. The long term Sharpe of the MVV/UST/UBT approach is also expected to be higher, so for those seeking to have larger risk adjusted returns – even if this means some lowering of returns – this might also be a good option.

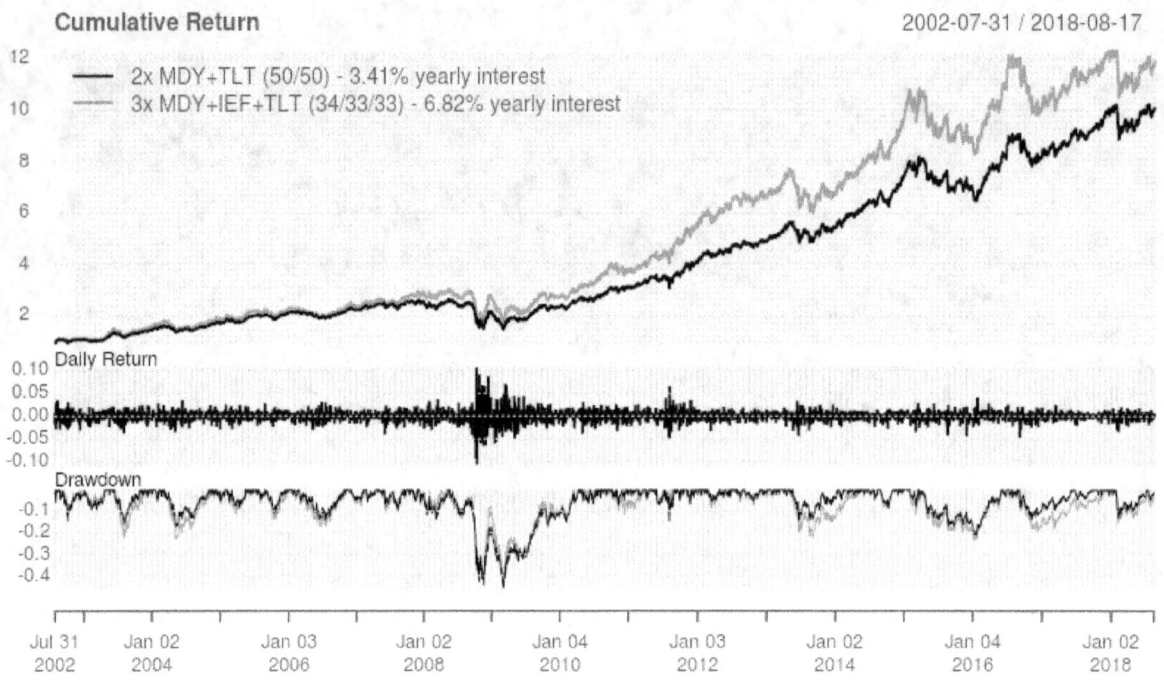

Figure 14: Comparison between 2x MDY/TLT and 3x MDY/TLT/IEF approaches

Notice that I also included MVV in Figure 13 to show you that the past 8 years have been a remarkably bullish period for stocks and both of these portfolios would have under-performed the simple leveraged index ETF heavily. However you can see in the drawdown plot that the risks our portfolios took were much lower than those of the index ETF and we therefore expect our setups to perform much better under crisis situations. It is worth noting that you should never judge performance solely on graphs that have not shown significant market cycling – like the past 8 years – as you are bound to come to erroneous conclusions that might encourage you to take excessive risks. When taking something like this to a 30+ year period – as we did when we used mutual funds to expand our historical view – we could see how a leveraged stock/bond portfolio can perform significantly better than a simple stock buy-and-hold trading approach.

However since the combination of MDY/TLT/IEF increases risk adjusted returns we can actually use more leverage to take advantage of this and see if we can obtain even better returns without more risk. We can do this by hypothesizing a 3x leveraged scenario with daily rebalancing where we pay a 6.82% yearly interest on margin. The results of doing this – shown in Figure 14 – reveal that an increase to 3x leverage when using an equally distributed MDY/TLT/IEF portfolio does seem to pay off. Actually in this case we increase our annualized returns to 16.49% Vs 15.36% and we actually even decrease our maximum drawdown from 45.40% to 42.75%.

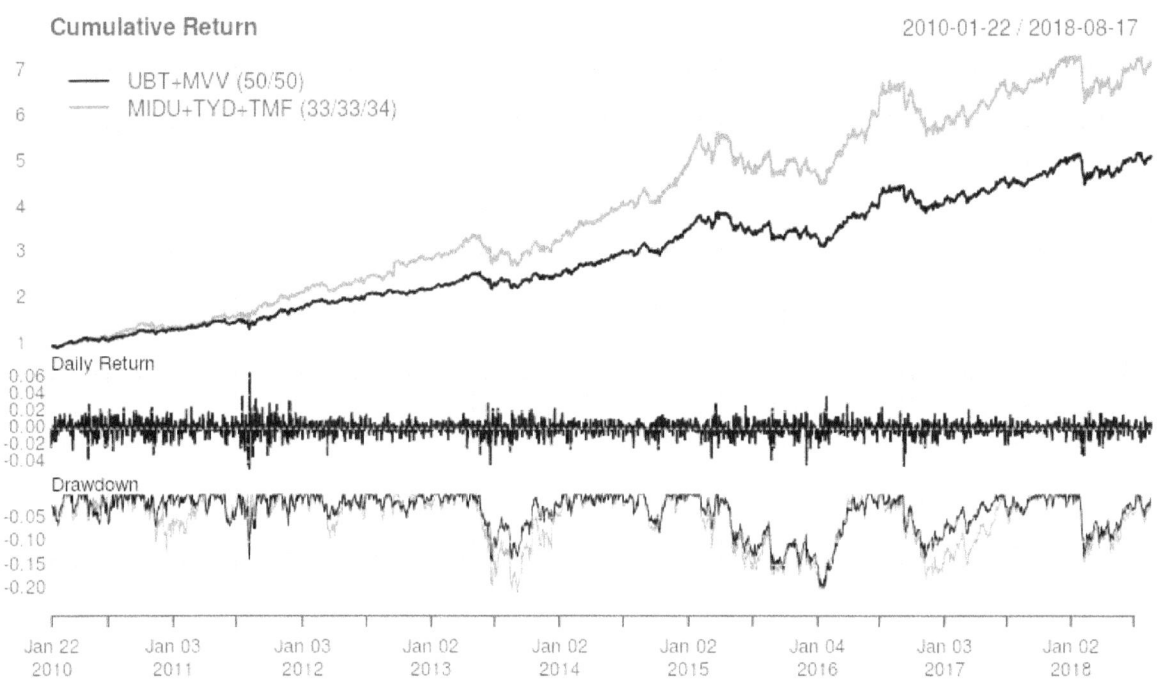

Figure 15: Comparison between UBT/MVV and MIDU/TYD/TMF portfolios

We could actually reproduce such a 3x leverage approach using the MIDU (3x S&P Mid Cap 400), TYD (3x 7-10 year government bonds) and TMF (3x 20+ year government bonds) ETFs. Figure 15 shows you the comparison between the results of this portfolio and our MVV/UBT portfolio, which uses 2x leverage. The returns during the past ten years are indeed much larger for our MIDU/TYD/TMF portfolio, which an average return of 25.60% against the 20.80% return of the MVV/UBT case. Our maximum drawdown is however larger in this case – although not by much – having reached a 20.73% loss versus a 19.63% loss for MVV/UBT. The Sharpe ratios for the two portfolios are fairly similar (1.33 Vs 1.29) although in this case our new 3x leveraged portfolio did manage to beat our 2x portfolio by a small margin.

These results show you how we can indeed include shorter term government bonds – that have a naturally lower volatility – and we can make even higher returning portfolios by increasing the leverage of our approach even further. We showed how the 2x leveraged approach using these bonds can lead to much better Sharpes – with lower returns – with the 3x leveraged approach having very similar historical risk characteristics and yet better returns than our 2x leveraged approach. We went through synthetic results using hypothetically leveraged portfolios from 2002 and we also saw how these approaches translate into actually tradeable scenarios using 3x leveraged ETF products.

It is also important to mention that the universe of bonds available is very large and there could be a myriad of potential combinations with better historical results compared to the above. However the amount of leveraged long bond ETFs available is small and we are therefore limited in our ability to do leveraged passive investing if we're focused on the use of instruments that already incorporate leverage in order to save trading costs. An obvious approach to protect ourselves from inflation – for example – would be to use inflation-protected bonds (the TIP ETF tracks their performance) but it turns out that there are currently no TIP based leveraged products, making this a nonviable strategy for us.

If you're willing to take a margin-based approach to using leverage then the amount of options you could explore becomes much bigger but I have decided to keep the portfolios explored in this book limited to implicit leverage approaches as I know that these are easy to actually execute by most investors as they do not require any extensive management (like daily rebalancing of leverage) which can be problematic for someone who wants the investment to be as truly passive as possible.

Monitoring portfolios and timing investments

As I mentioned within the introduction this section is not necessary to take advantage of the knowledge within this book. Within the past section you've already learned how to construct leveraged passive income portfolios with excellent market returns and you can use this information to invest without any further complications. However this chapter will provide you with additional insights that – if you are inclined to invest a little time – may help you better time your investments to maximize your potential long term returns.

Analyzing your portfolio

In this section we are going to go deeper into how we can analyze our leveraged portfolios in order to track their performance through time and eventually maximize our potential returns even further. To do this we are going to use the R Studio software to track portfolio returns and drawdown on an on-going basis.

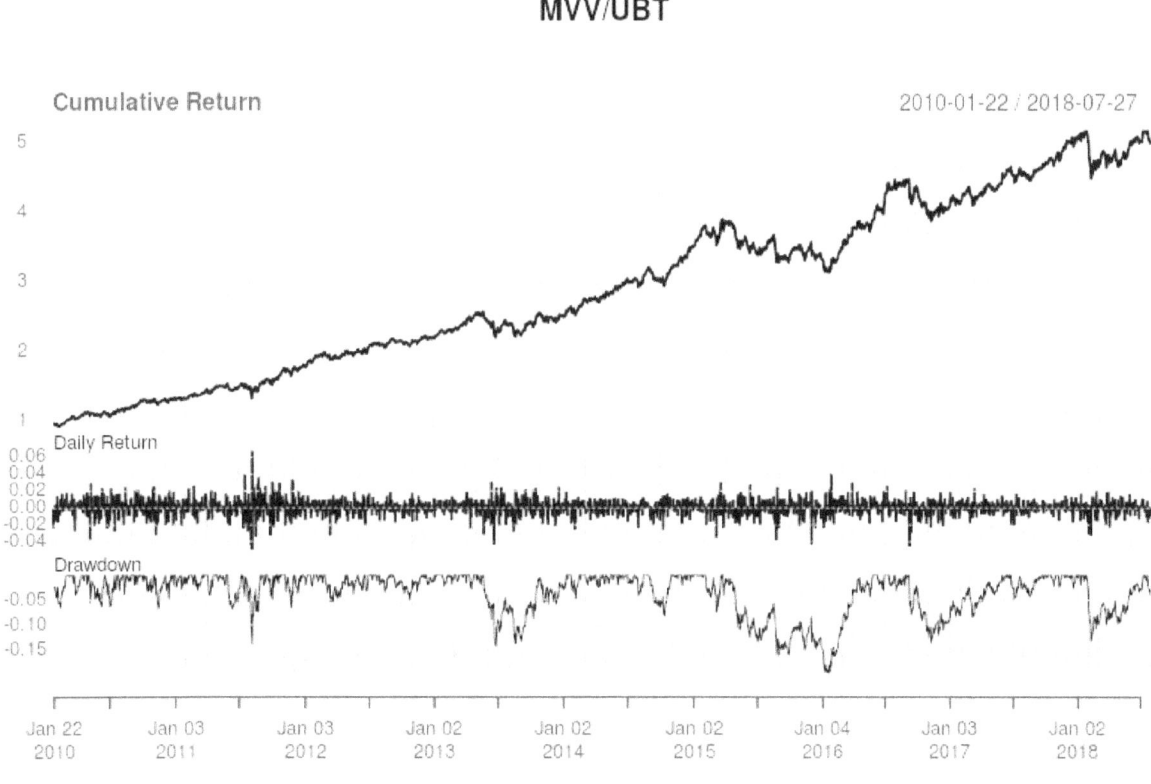

Figure 16: Current all-time MVV/UBT historical graph

By using R we will be able to tell whether a given portfolio is currently underwater or not and whether it is a good time or not to invest in it. You will find all the code needed for this under the "Figure 16-18" heading in the R code appendix. With this code you will be able to reproduce all the graphs and statistics shown within this chapter. We will be using the MVV/UBT portfolio as an example.

The first thing we will learn to do is generate the all-history MVV/UBT graph. This graph, shown in Figure 16, is generated by first obtaining the entire history of the two symbols using the getSymbols function from the quantmod library and then using the "charts.PerformanceSummary" function from the PerformanceAnalytics library.

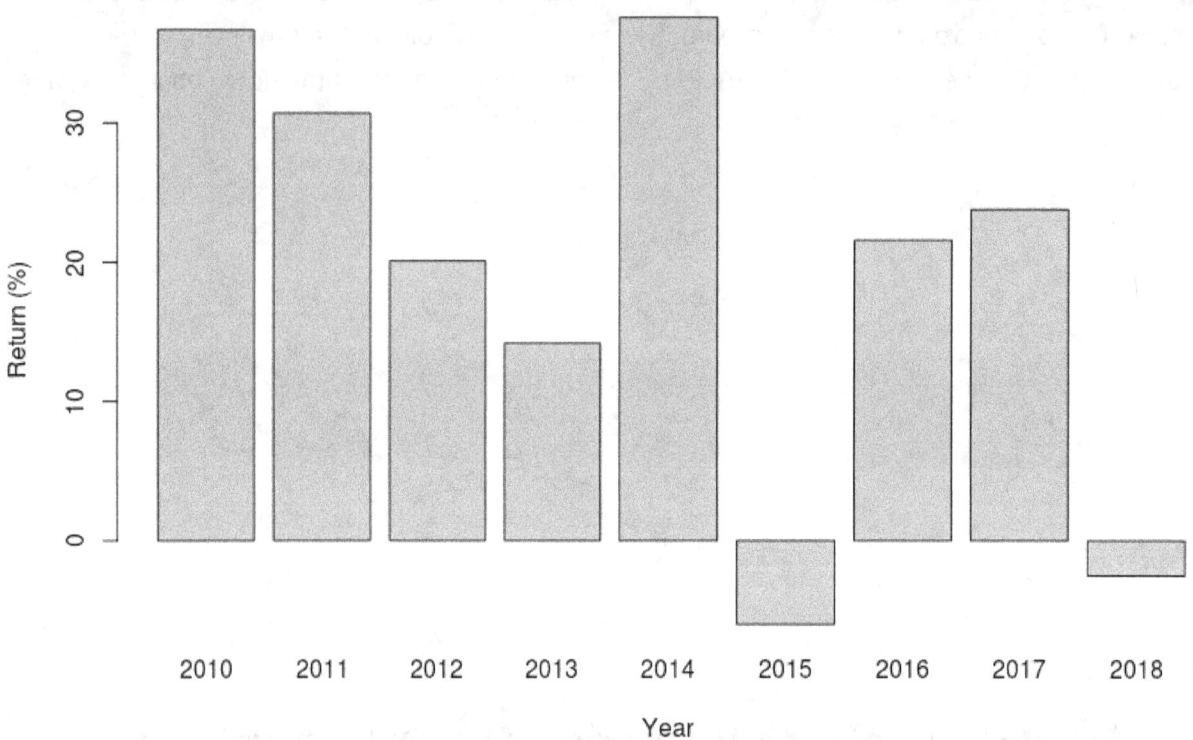

Figure 17: Yearly return values for the MVV/UBT portfolio

In addition to this graph we might want to obtain a yearly performance graph in order to get an idea of how the yearly return can vary for our specific portfolio – which can help us see how normal or abnormal the current year is – in order to do this we should convert our prices to monthly instead of daily returns and then use the "table.CalendarReturns" function to obtain a table that shows us yearly and monthly performance for the portfolio. Using this table and the "barplot" function we can then display the yearly performance for our portfolio, as shown in Figure 17.

We can also easily select some smaller period of time by adjusting the "from" value in the getSymbols call that we use to obtain the data. Changing this value to 2018 allows us to obtain the graph seen in Figure 18.

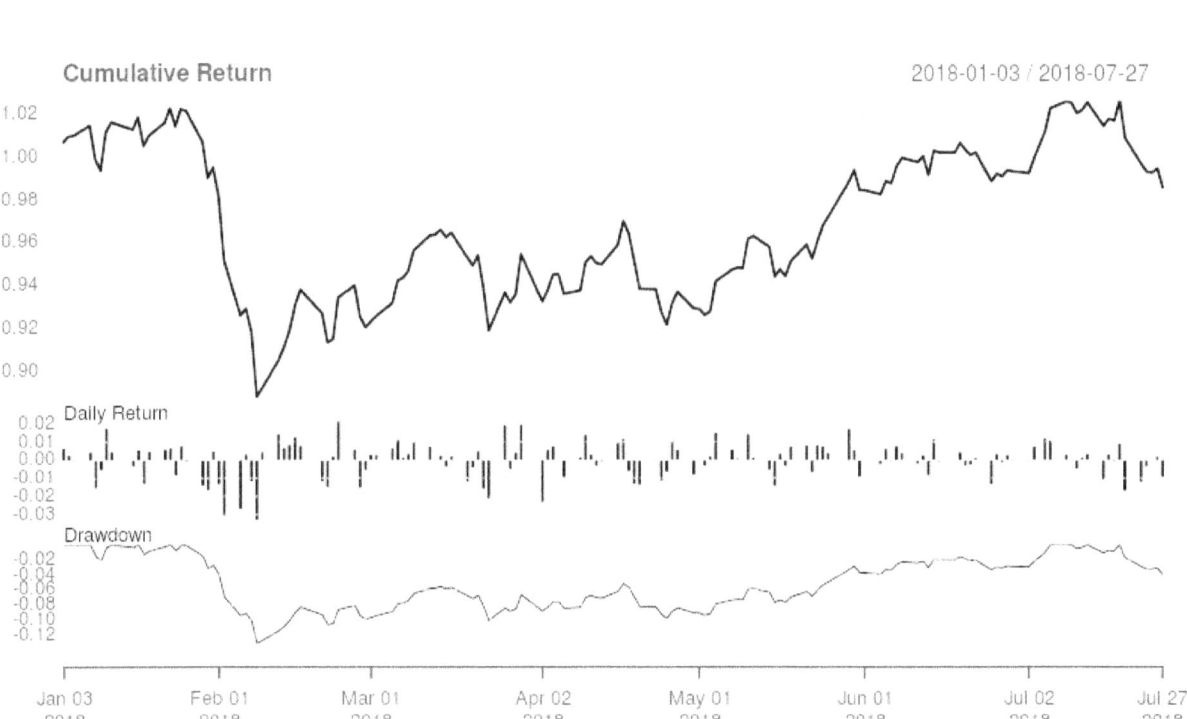

Figure 18: Results for an MVV/UBT portfolio in 2018 up to July

Note that using this shorter span gives us a clearer image of where we are in the short term. We can see that performance for the portfolio has been negative for the year so far and we can also see that at the end of July we are currently close to a 4% drawdown.

Although we can deduce all of this from the graph it would also be useful to be able to obtain actual numbers for these figures. Using the "Return.cumulative", "maxDrawdown" and "Drawdowns" functions we can also obtain the current total return, maximum drawdown and data for the underwater plot for our portfolio. In general I like to call the "Drawdowns" function inside a "tail" function call in order to just see the last 5 data points. In this particular case the cumulative return for this portfolio for 2018 is -1.47%, the maximum drawdown is 13.14% and the current drawdown value is -3.9% (last value in the "Drawdowns" function call). This corroborates the information seen in both Figures 16 and 17. From this we know that 2018 was a losing year up until the end of July and that the portfolio was at a drawdown period at this specific point in time.

Drawdowns and investing

Since we are investing in instruments that are bound to increase in value as a function of time – bonds and stocks – we should therefore be confident in the ability of these instruments to recover from drawdown periods. This means that we expect all loses to be temporary and we should therefore view them as discount opportunities – times to buy cheap – instead of times to panic. However we shouldn't be waiting all the time for large drops in order to invest because this might make us miss very significant periods of market growth having our money sitting on the sidelines.

In general I practice an approach where I avoid investing at new all-time highs since we are almost guaranteed to have some level of drawdown within a given time period. We can calculate the percentage of the time that a portfolio spends below a given drawdown level, which can give us an idea of how frequent or infrequent such opportunities are to invest. The "Figure 19" code in the R code appendix contains 3 lines that show you how this is calculated for 5%, 10% and 15% drawdowns for our example portfolio. It also contains a few lines that allow you to plot the frequency distribution shown in Figure 19.

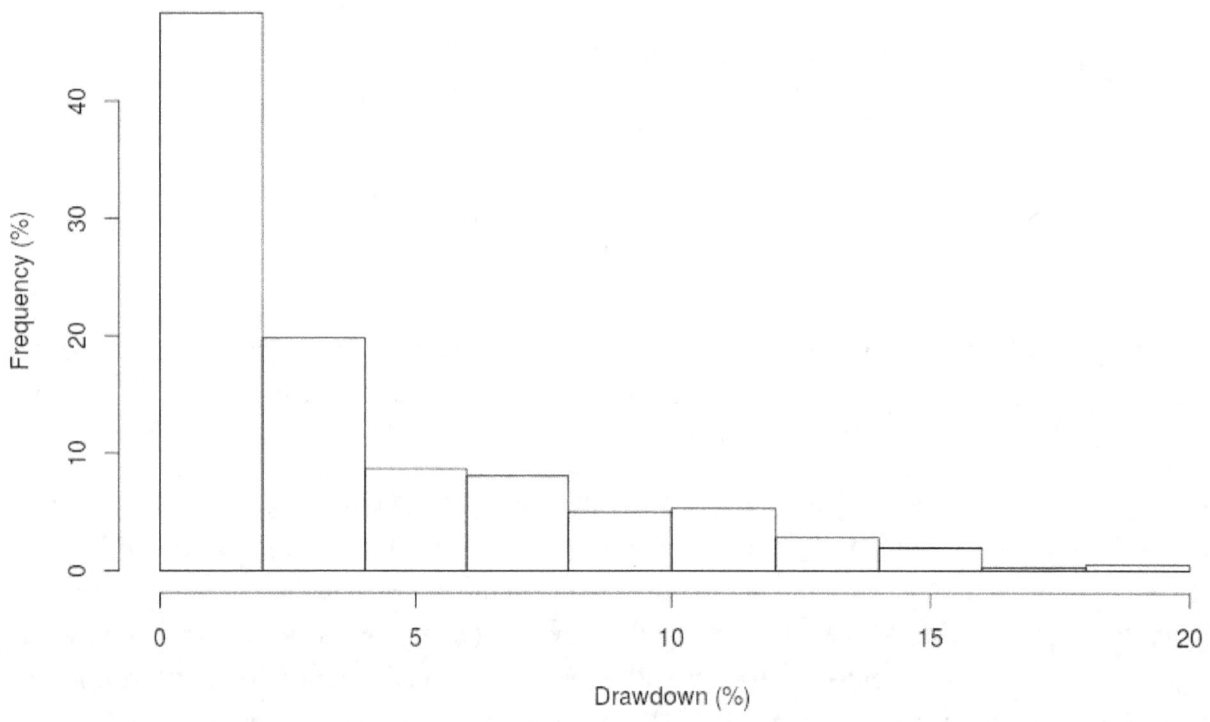

Figure 19: Frequency distribution for drawdown levels in the MVV/UBT portfolio

In the case of MVV/UBT since 2010 the portfolio has spent 28.21% of days at a drawdown at or greater than 5% - what you obtained if you added the 5% and higher boxes in Figure 19 –, 10.9% of the time at a drawdown at or greater than 10% and only 1.63% of the time at a drawdown at or greater than 15%. This means that although there are some great opportunities to buy at a 15% discount from time to time, they are likely to be difficult to catch and might lead us to waste an important amount of growth waiting for "the right time". However it is clear that we spend almost a third of the time at a drawdown at or greater than 5% so waiting for some time to invest when the portfolio is losing at least 5% is a good way to maximize our potential profits. You can change the numbers in these lines to calculate values for any given drawdown depths you want.

Most investors approach the market using dollar cost averaging – investing in portfolios consistently over time regardless of how the market is behaving – but this approach is heavily sub-optimal considering that returns can be enhanced tremendously if we just wait a little bit for frequent drawdown numbers to come up. Depending on the risk level of your portfolio you might need to wait for shallower or deeper drawdowns but in essence you can use a simple historical analysis to get an idea of how frequent a given drawdown level is and choose a level that is expected to happen with some high relative frequency in order to time your overall investments well. It is always wise to avoid investing at new all-time highs as portfolios are guaranteed to go into shallow drawdowns with enough frequency to make these temporary discounts an extremely good opportunity for long term investors.

I do this instead of waiting for very deep infrequent drawdowns both because this might mean missing out on long periods of very-stable trading with significant growth and because investing in these periods is also particularly challenging from a psychological perspective. Although it would be mathematically optimal to invest every penny when the portfolio is at a 40% drawdown you would need to potentially wait for decades and you would need to invest when everyone is panicking (which most investors are unlikely to do). Instead investing within shallow frequent drawdowns enhances your compounding to a big extent without putting you in a psychologically hard spot.

In general I perform portfolio analysis every single day – by executing a few lines of R code – and I decide with this information whether it is a good time to enter with new investment capital. If I have money to invest I place it in my brokerage account and I enter the market whenever I have a day where the portfolio exceeds my target drawdown threshold. I therefore always only buy when there is some discount in price, which greatly enhanced my ability to compound returns. Think about it as only buying an item at the grocery store when it is on sale, knowing the item you want will be on sale almost one third of the time!

Notes about risk and risk tolerance

It is one thing to see a 50% drawdown on a chart and an entirely different thing to live it. The portfolios mentioned within this book assume for the most part that you're willing to take the same level of risk as a naked stock index investment but this level of risk is significantly high in any case. Within these periods it is important to remember that the portfolios within this book are based on investments that are all expected to increase in value in the long term and that these types of set backs are bound to happen. These portfolios are built on strong, long term relationships between stocks and bonds and are meant to respond well to a wide variety of market conditions.

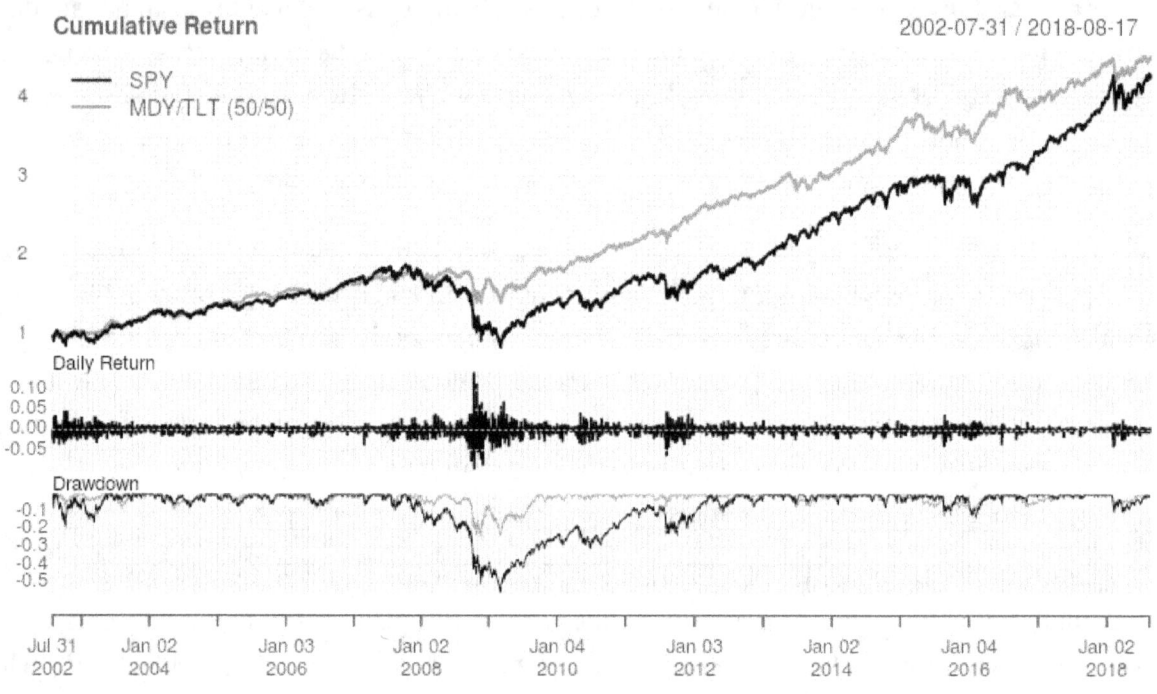

Figure 20: Comparison between the SPY and an MDY/TLT portfolio

Of course I cannot guarantee that the future will be the same as the past and that the relationships between low risk bonds and stocks will remain the same but we have seen evidence of how these relationships have behaved in the long term, including several different periods when market turmoil stroke. Under all of these circumstances the investments went into deep periods of temporary losses that were then recovered and selling our shares in any of these periods would have been a terrible mistake. In the same manner as selling a naked stock index investment in a market downturn is the worst possible idea, these portfolios are meant to be treated as long term investments and should not be sold when these foreseen deep drawdown periods strike.

If you're not comfortable with this level of loss and you would prefer to get close to stock index returns with reduced risks, then you can perform investments like a 50/50 MDY/TLT portfolio – which you can see in Figure 19 – without any leverage. This portfolio has exceeded the performance of an index like the SPY since 2002. In this particular case the return of MDY/TLT was 9.7% while that of the SPY was 9.4%. In this case the maximum drawdown was 23.67% for the portfolio while for the SPY it was 55.18%.

Note that the objective of our leveraged portfolios is to greatly enhance our long term performance at what is usually considered an acceptable level of risk – the naked stock market index exposure – but we can certainly use the stock/bond relationships to lower risk to achieve stock index like performance. Depending on your risk tolerance and age you should choose whichever approach is more appropriate.

Conclusions

Within this book we have seen how we can construct leveraged passive investing portfolios using leveraged ETF instruments. We have seen how we can use leverage and the relationships between bonds and stocks to not only increase returns but to also decrease risk relative to simple stock index investments. Figure 21 shows you what we have been able to achieve using the 2x and 3x approaches we described within previous chapters and how this compares to a SPY investment.

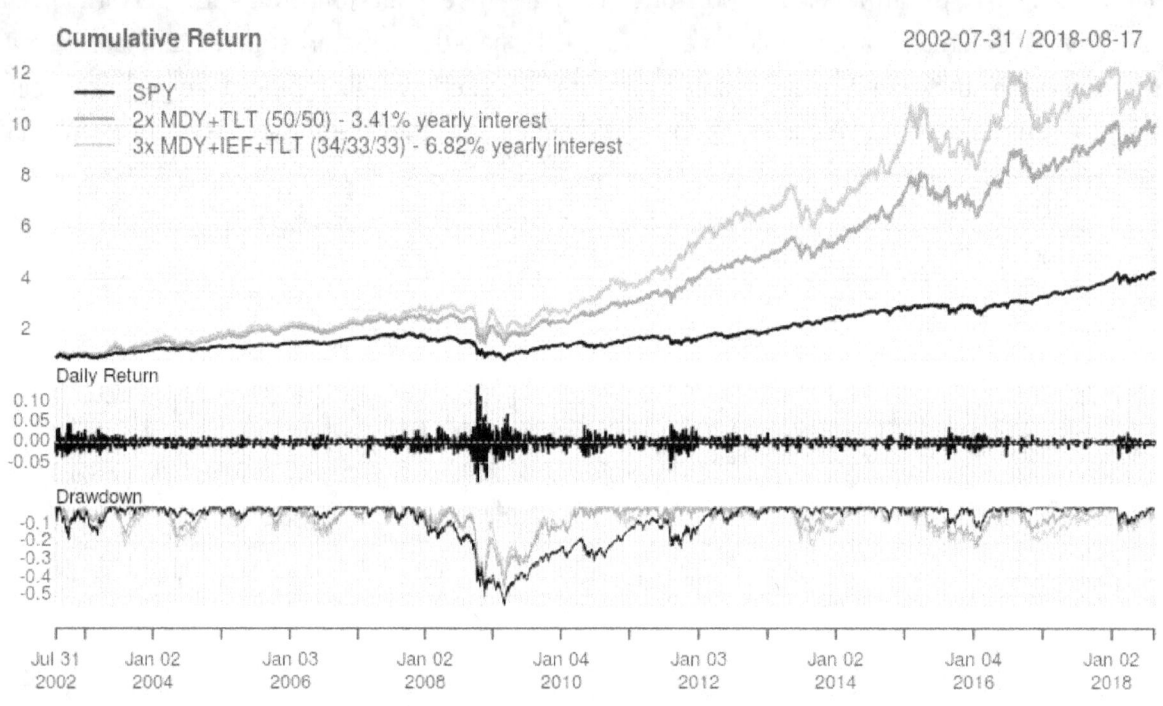

Figure 21: Comparison between the SPY and 2x and 3x leveraged portfolios using MDY, IEF and TLT

During the 2002-2018 period our leveraged portfolios were able to make average annualized returns of 15.36% and 16.49% compared to the SPY's return of 9.46%. We can do this while reducing our maximum drawdown from 55.18% in the SPY to either 45.40% or 42.75%, depending on the type of portfolio used. Our Sharpe ratio also increases sharply from the 0.51 of the SPY to 0.77 and 0.73 respectively. It is also worth noting that the above graph shows MDY/TLT and MDY/IEF/TLT leveraged approaches paying interest on margin so we would expect the MVV/UBT and MIDU/TYD/TMF portfolios to be cheaper and therefore yield even better returns and risk adjusted characteristics compared to these hypothetical references going forward.

This book also showed you how you can better time your investments to achieve even higher returns using these portfolios by following the present-day drawdown levels of the portfolios and choosing to enter the market with new investments whenever a frequently expected drawdown mark is reached.

I hope that this book has provided you with good ideas about how you can increase your long term returns without needing to be extremely active in trading and without having to spend a ton of time studying the markets. I also hope this book has showed you that leverage is not necessarily the extremely dangerous and unpredictable thing many people point it out to be but that with an understanding of what is being done one can expect to use this great tool to maximize the potential of financial instruments that would otherwise have very low volatility or returns (like for example 7-10 year US government bonds). This book shows how very simple 2 and 3 instrument portfolios with very simple assumptions have in the past greatly increased returns and often reduced risk relative to more commonly recommended investment strategies.

I use these strategies within my personal trading and with them hope to achieve a long term 15-20% return rate, which will greatly increase my long term profits relative to a naked stock index investment. Although the assumptions within this book are certainly not without risk, I hope that this book has opened up your mind to the idea of understanding leverage and the ways in which it can be used to increase returns, even for passive investment strategies.

R code appendix

This section provides the R code used to create all the figures within this book. The code always requests data up to present date so as time passes new data – that is not shown in the graphs within this book – will appear on your charts. Make sure you always execute the first two lines – which load the quantmod and PerformanceAnalytics libraries – before executing any other piece of code. The code for each figure is meant to be independent so you can obtain each figure by just executing the code in R for it. Note that figures will be in color and not in the gray scale used for the book, this way you will probably find them easier to read.

```
library(quantmod)
library(PerformanceAnalytics)

#Figure 1
getSymbols(c("SPY"),src="yahoo", from="1993-01-01")
SPY <- Delt(SPY$SPY.Adjusted)
colnames(SPY) <- c("SPY")
charts.PerformanceSummary(SPY, ylog=TRUE)
Return.annualized(SPY)
maxDrawdown(SPY)
SharpeRatio.annualized(SPY)


getSymbols(c("DIA"),src="yahoo", from="1993-01-01")
DIA<- Delt(DIA$DIA.Adjusted)
colnames(DIA) <- c("DIA")
charts.PerformanceSummary(DIA, ylog=TRUE)
Return.annualized(DIA)
maxDrawdown(DIA)
SharpeRatio.annualized(DIA)

p <- na.omit(merge(DIA,SPY))
colnames(p) <- c("DIA","SPY")
Return.annualized(p)
maxDrawdown(p)
SharpeRatio.annualized(p)

#Figure 2

getSymbols(c("SPY"),src="yahoo", from="2015-01-01")
SPY <- na.omit(Delt(SPY$SPY.Adjusted))
SPY_2x <- Delt(2*cumprod(1+SPY)-1.0)

interest <- 0.0341/252
SPY_2x_i <- SPY
for (i in 1:length(SPY_2x_i)){
  if (i == 1){
    SPY_2x_i[i] <- 2
```

```r
  } else {
    SPY_2x_i[i] <- SPY_2x_i$Delt.1.arithmetic[[i-1]]
+SPY$Delt.1.arithmetic[[i]]*SPY_2x_i$Delt.1.arithmetic[[i-1]]-interest
  }
}
SPY_2x_i <-Delt(SPY_2x_i - 1.0)

p <- na.omit(merge(SPY, SPY_2x, SPY_2x_i))
colnames(p) <- c("SPY", "2x SPY", "2x SPY - 3.41% annual interest")
charts.PerformanceSummary(p, ylog=TRUE,main="SPY, 2x SPY and 2x SPY plus cost")
Return.annualized(p)

#Figure 3

getSymbols(c("SPY"),src="yahoo", from="1993-01-01")
SPY <- na.omit(Delt(SPY$SPY.Adjusted))

interest <- 0.0341/252
SPY_2x_i <- SPY
for (i in 1:length(SPY_2x_i)){
  if (i == 1){
    SPY_2x_i[i] <- 2
  } else {
    SPY_2x_i[i] <- SPY_2x_i$Delt.1.arithmetic[[i-1]]
+SPY$Delt.1.arithmetic[[i]]*SPY_2x_i$Delt.1.arithmetic[[i-1]]-interest
  }
}
SPY_2x_i <-Delt(SPY_2x_i - 1.0)

p <- na.omit(merge(SPY, 2*SPY-interest, SPY_2x_i))
colnames(p) <- c("SPY", "2x SPY daily rebalancing", "2x SPY no rebalancing")
charts.PerformanceSummary(p, ylog=TRUE,main="SPY and 2x SPY with and without rebalancing")
Return.annualized(p)

#Figure 4

getSymbols(c("SPY", "SSO"),src="yahoo", from="1993-01-01")
SPY <- Delt(SPY$SPY.Adjusted)
SSO <- Delt(SSO$SSO.Adjusted)
interest <- 0.0341/252
p <- na.omit(merge(SPY, 2*SPY-interest, SSO))
colnames(p) <- c("SPY", "2x SPY - 3.41% annual interest", "SSO")
charts.PerformanceSummary(p, ylog=TRUE,main="Implied leverage Vs Margin leverage comparison",legend.loc="top")
Return.cumulative(p)
maxDrawdown(p)

#Figure 5
```

```r
getSymbols(c("SPY", "SSO"),src="yahoo", from="2018-01-01")
SPY <- Delt(SPY$SPY.Adjusted)
SSO <- Delt(SSO$SSO.Adjusted)
p <- merge(SPY, SSO)
colnames(p) <- c("SPY", "SSO")
charts.PerformanceSummary(p, ylog=TRUE,main="SPY Vs SSO
Performance",legend.loc="top")
Return.cumulative(p)
maxDrawdown(p)

#Figure 6
getSymbols(c("VUSTX", "VFINX"),src="yahoo", from="1986-01-01")
VUSTX <- Delt(VUSTX$VUSTX.Adjusted)
VFINX <- Delt(VFINX$VFINX.Adjusted)
p <- na.omit(merge(VUSTX, VFINX, VUSTX*0.5+VFINX*0.5))
colnames(p) <- c("VUSTX", "VFINX", "VUSTX+VFINX portfolio (50/50)")
charts.PerformanceSummary(p, ylog=TRUE,main="VUSTX, VFINX and VUSTX+VFINX 50/50
portfolio")
Return.annualized(p)
maxDrawdown(p)
SharpeRatio.annualized(p)
Return.cumulative(p)

#Figure 7
getSymbols(c("VUSTX", "VFINX"),src="yahoo", from="1986-01-01")
VUSTX <- Delt(VUSTX$VUSTX.Adjusted)
VFINX <- Delt(VFINX$VFINX.Adjusted)
interest <- 0.0341/252
p <- na.omit(merge(VUSTX*0.5+VFINX*0.5, 2*(VUSTX*0.5+VFINX*0.5)-interest))
colnames(p) <- c("VUSTX+VFINX portfolio (50/50)", "2x VUSTX+VFINX portfolio
(50/50) - 3.41% yearly interest")
charts.PerformanceSummary(p, ylog=TRUE,main="VUSTX/VFINX unleveraged and leveraged
portfolios")
Return.annualized(p)
maxDrawdown(p)
SharpeRatio.annualized(p)
Return.cumulative(p)

#Figure 8
getSymbols(c("VUSTX", "VFINX","SSO","UBT"),src="yahoo", from="1986-01-01")
VUSTX <- Delt(VUSTX$VUSTX.Adjusted)
VFINX <- Delt(VFINX$VFINX.Adjusted)
UBT <- Delt(UBT$UBT.Adjusted)
SSO <- Delt(SSO$SSO.Adjusted)
interest <- 0.0341/252
p <- na.omit(merge(0.5*UBT+0.5*SSO, 2*(VUSTX*0.5+VFINX*0.5)-interest))
colnames(p) <- c("UBT+SSO (50/50)", "2x VUSTX+VFINX portfolio (50/50) - 3.41%
yearly interest")
charts.PerformanceSummary(p, ylog=TRUE,main="VUSTX/VFINX leveraged vs SSO/UBT
portfolios")
```

```
Return.annualized(p)
maxDrawdown(p)
SharpeRatio.annualized(p)
Return.cumulative(p)

#Figure 9
getSymbols(c("MVV","SSO","UBT"),src="yahoo", from="1986-01-01")
MVV <- Delt(MVV$MVV.Adjusted)
UBT <- Delt(UBT$UBT.Adjusted)
SSO <- Delt(SSO$SSO.Adjusted)
p <- na.omit(merge(0.5*UBT+0.5*SSO, 0.5*UBT+0.5*MVV))
colnames(p) <- c("UBT+SSO (50/50)", "UBT+MVV (50/50)")
charts.PerformanceSummary(p, ylog=TRUE,main="MVV/UBT vs SSO/UBT portfolios")
Return.annualized(p)
maxDrawdown(p)
SharpeRatio.annualized(p)
Return.cumulative(p)

#Figure 10
getSymbols(c("VUSTX", "VFINX","VIMSX"),src="yahoo", from="1986-01-01")
VUSTX <- Delt(VUSTX$VUSTX.Adjusted)
VFINX <- Delt(VFINX$VFINX.Adjusted)
VIMSX <- Delt(VIMSX$VIMSX.Adjusted)
interest <- 0.0341/252
p <- na.omit(merge(2*(VUSTX*0.5+VFINX*0.5)-interest,2*(VUSTX*0.5+VIMSX*0.5)-
interest))
colnames(p) <- c("2x VUSTX+VFINX portfolio (50/50) - 3.41% yearly interest", "2x
VUSTX+VIMSX portfolio (50/50) - 3.41% yearly interest")
charts.PerformanceSummary(p, ylog=TRUE,main="Leveraged VUSTX/VFINX vs VUSTX/VIMSX
portfolios")
Return.annualized(p)
maxDrawdown(p)
SharpeRatio.annualized(p)
Return.cumulative(p)

#Figure 11
getSymbols(c("SAA","SSO","UBT"),src="yahoo", from="1986-01-01")
SAA <- Delt(SAA$SAA.Adjusted)
UBT <- Delt(UBT$UBT.Adjusted)
SSO <- Delt(SSO$SSO.Adjusted)
p <- na.omit(merge(0.5*UBT+0.5*SSO, 0.5*UBT+0.5*SAA))
colnames(p) <- c("UBT+SSO (50/50)", "UBT+SAA (50/50)")
charts.PerformanceSummary(p, ylog=TRUE,main="SAA/UBT vs SSO/UBT portfolios")
Return.annualized(p)
maxDrawdown(p)
SharpeRatio.annualized(p)
Return.cumulative(p)

#Figure 12
getSymbols(c("MDY","IEF","TLT"),src="yahoo", from="1986-01-01")
```

```
MDY <- Delt(MDY$MDY.Adjusted)
IEF <- Delt(IEF$IEF.Adjusted)
TLT <- Delt(TLT$TLT.Adjusted)
interest <- 0.0341/252
p1 <- 2*(MDY*0.5+TLT*0.5)-interest
p2 <- 2*(MDY*0.5+IEF*0.5)-interest
p3 <- 2*(MDY*0.5+IEF*0.25+TLT*0.25)-interest
p4 <- 2*(MDY*0.34+IEF*0.33+TLT*0.33)-interest
p <- na.omit(merge(p1,p2,p3,p4))
colnames(p) <- c("2x MDY+TLT (50/50) - 3.41% yearly interest", "2x MDY+IEF(50/50) - 3.41% yearly interest", "2x MDY+IEF+TLT (50/25/25) - 3.41% yearly interest", "2x MDY+IEF+TLT (34/33/33) - 3.41% yearly interest")
charts.PerformanceSummary(p, ylog=TRUE,main="MDY,TLT,IEF portfolios")
Return.annualized(p)
maxDrawdown(p)
SharpeRatio.annualized(p)
Return.cumulative(p)

#Figure 13
getSymbols(c("MVV","UST","UBT"),src="yahoo", from="1986-01-01")
MVV <- Delt(MVV$MVV.Adjusted)
UBT <- Delt(UBT$UBT.Adjusted)
UST <- Delt(UST$UST.Adjusted)
p <- na.omit(merge(MVV, 0.5*UBT+0.5*MVV, 0.34*MVV+0.33*UBT+0.33*UST))
colnames(p) <- c("MVV", "UBT+MVV (50/50)", "UBT+UST+MVV (33/33/34)")
charts.PerformanceSummary(p, ylog=TRUE,main="MVV/UBT/UST portfolios")
Return.annualized(p)
maxDrawdown(p)
SharpeRatio.annualized(p)
Return.cumulative(p)

#Figure 14
getSymbols(c("MDY","IEF","TLT"),src="yahoo", from="1986-01-01")
MDY <- Delt(MDY$MDY.Adjusted)
IEF <- Delt(IEF$IEF.Adjusted)
TLT <- Delt(TLT$TLT.Adjusted)
interest <- 0.0341/252
p1 <- 2*(MDY*0.5+TLT*0.5)-interest
p2 <- 3*(MDY*0.34+IEF*0.33+TLT*0.33)-interest*2
p <- na.omit(merge(p1,p2))
colnames(p) <- c("2x MDY+TLT (50/50) - 3.41% yearly interest", "3x MDY+IEF+TLT (34/33/33) - 6.82% yearly interest")
charts.PerformanceSummary(p, ylog=TRUE,main="MDY,TLT,IEF portfolios")
Return.annualized(p)
maxDrawdown(p)
SharpeRatio.annualized(p)
Return.cumulative(p)

#Figure 15
getSymbols(c("MVV","TYD","TMF","UBT","MIDU"),src="yahoo", from="1986-01-01")
```

```
MVV <- Delt(MVV$MVV.Adjusted)
TYD <- Delt(TYD$TYD.Adjusted)
TMF <- Delt(TMF$TMF.Adjusted)
UBT <- Delt(UBT$UBT.Adjusted)
MIDU <- Delt(MIDU$MIDU.Adjusted)
p <- na.omit(merge(0.5*UBT+0.5*MVV, 0.34*MIDU+0.33*TYD+0.33*TMF))
colnames(p) <- c("UBT+MVV (50/50)", "MIDU+TYD+TMF (33/33/34)")
charts.PerformanceSummary(p, ylog=TRUE,main="MVV/UBT Vs MIDU/TYD/TMF portfolios")
Return.annualized(p)
maxDrawdown(p)
SharpeRatio.annualized(p)
Return.cumulative(p)

#Figure 16
getSymbols(c("MVV","UBT"),src="yahoo", from="1986-01-01")
MVV <- Delt(MVV$MVV.Adjusted)
UBT <- Delt(UBT$UBT.Adjusted)
p <- na.omit(merge(0.5*UBT+0.5*MVV))
colnames(p) <- c("UBT+MVV (50/50)")
charts.PerformanceSummary(p, ylog=TRUE,main="MVV/UBT")


#Figure 17
getSymbols(c("MVV","UBT"),src="yahoo", from="1986-01-01")
MVV <- monthlyReturn(MVV$MVV.Adjusted)
UBT <- monthlyReturn(UBT$UBT.Adjusted)
p <- na.omit(merge(0.5*UBT+0.5*MVV))
colnames(p) <- c("UBT+MVV (50/50)")
yearly_returns <- table.CalendarReturns(p, as.perc=TRUE)
barplot(yearly_returns$"UBT+MVV (50/50)", names.arg=row.names(yearly_returns),
xlab="Year", ylab="Return (%)")

Figure #18
getSymbols(c("MVV","UBT"),src="yahoo", from="2018-01-01")
MVV <- Delt(MVV$MVV.Adjusted)
UBT <- Delt(UBT$UBT.Adjusted)
p <- na.omit(merge(0.5*UBT+0.5*MVV))
colnames(p) <- c("UBT+MVV (50/50)")
charts.PerformanceSummary(p, ylog=TRUE,main="MVV/UBT")
maxDrawdown(p)
Return.cumulative(p)
tail(Drawdowns(p), 5)

#Figure19
getSymbols(c("MVV","UBT"),src="yahoo", from="1986-01-01")
MVV <- Delt(MVV$MVV.Adjusted)
UBT <- Delt(UBT$UBT.Adjusted)
p <- na.omit(merge(0.5*UBT+0.5*MVV))
colnames(p) <- c("UBT+MVV (50/50)")
h = hist(-100.0*Drawdowns(p)$"UBT+MVV (50/50)")
```

```r
h$density = h$counts/sum(h$counts)*100
plot(h,freq=FALSE, xlab="Drawdown (%)", ylab="Frequency (%)", main="Frequencies for different drawdown levels")

length(Drawdowns(p)[Drawdowns(p)$"UBT+MVV (50/50)" < -0.05,])/length(Drawdowns(p)$"UBT+MVV (50/50)")
length(Drawdowns(p)[Drawdowns(p)$"UBT+MVV (50/50)" < -0.10,])/length(Drawdowns(p)$"UBT+MVV (50/50)")
length(Drawdowns(p)[Drawdowns(p)$"UBT+MVV (50/50)" < -0.15,])/length(Drawdowns(p)$"UBT+MVV (50/50)")

#Figure 20
getSymbols(c("MDY","TLT", "SPY"),src="yahoo", from="1986-01-01")
SPY <- Delt(SPY$SPY.Adjusted)
MDY <- Delt(MDY$MDY.Adjusted)
TLT <- Delt(TLT$TLT.Adjusted)
interest <- 0.0341/252
p <- na.omit(merge(SPY,MDY*0.5+TLT*0.5))
colnames(p) <- c("SPY", "MDY/TLT (50/50)")
charts.PerformanceSummary(p, ylog=TRUE,main="SPY vs MDY/TLT portfolio")
Return.annualized(p)
maxDrawdown(p)
SharpeRatio.annualized(p)
Return.cumulative(p)


#Figure 21
getSymbols(c("MDY","IEF","TLT"),src="yahoo", from="1986-01-01")
MDY <- Delt(MDY$MDY.Adjusted)
IEF <- Delt(IEF$IEF.Adjusted)
TLT <- Delt(TLT$TLT.Adjusted)
SPY <- Delt(SPY$SPY.Adjusted)
interest <- 0.0341/252
p1 <- 2*(MDY*0.5+TLT*0.5)-interest
p2 <- 3*(MDY*0.34+IEF*0.33+TLT*0.33)-interest*2
p <- na.omit(merge(SPY,p1,p2))
colnames(p) <- c("SPY", "2x MDY+TLT (50/50) - 3.41% yearly interest", "3x MDY+IEF+TLT (34/33/33) - 6.82% yearly interest")
charts.PerformanceSummary(p, ylog=TRUE,main="MDY,TLT,IEF portfolios")
Return.annualized(p)
maxDrawdown(p)
SharpeRatio.annualized(p)
Return.cumulative(p)
```